GET OFF THE SYSTEM: MOVING FROM LACK TO ABUNDANCE

GET OFF THE SYSTEM: MOVING FROM LACK TO ABUNDANCE

Alton Jamison

Get Off The System: Moving From Lack To Abundance

Copyright © 2018 by Alton Jamison

Book design by Madhouse Design Inc.

Edited by Susanna K. Green

Published by Create Space

All rights reserved. No part of this book may be reproduced, stored or transmitted by any means-whether auditory, graphic, mechanical or electronic-without written permission from the publisher, except in the case of brief excerpts used in critical articles and reviews. Unauthorized reproduction of any part of this work is illegal and is punishable by law.

ISBN 978-0-692-18519-3

This book is dedicated to my loving wife, TaShawnda Jamison, who relentlessly pushed me into the light when I was stuck in the darkness on this project. Thank you for the endless prayers, continuous pep talks and helping me see God's plan for this book; and... for my life. You are better than I deserve.

My wonderful gifts from God; my children, Madison and Joshua Jamison. How your love has changed my life for the better. Madison, your infectious joy always reminds me to set my mind on things above. Joshua, your love reminds me to focus on things that matter. May this book serve as an eternal pillar in the God-filled legacy we are creating for the two of you. May we be the bridge for you two to cross over into a God ordained and purpose filled life of health, wealth and supernatural success.

Anyone who has ever struggled financially and could not see their way out. If you have ever been tired of being sick and tired and ready to quit. When it feels like your season will never come and you feel stuck in the rat race of life. When you always have more bills than money and do not see a way out. God gave me this book just for you.

Contents

Acknowledgements..6

Foreword..8

Introduction..10

God's Economy..14

God's Abundance..21

God's Entrepreneur..32

God's Labor...47

God's Blessing...59

God's Deliverance..67

God's Promise..117

Daily Financial Confession......................................121

Author Info..123

Acknowledgements

To Apostle Howell and Pastor Marzetta, thank you for being wonderful leaders and spiritual parents. Apostle, I am honored to have you write the foreword for this work.

To Apostle White, Pastor White and the Abounding Love Church Family; thank you for always welcoming our family and allowing me to share my gifts in your space.

To Wallace King, thanks for another great cover! It is always a pleasure working for you.

To Teresa Brooks, a wonderful Realtor, wealth coach and the first person who taught me about multiple streams of income.

Ray Linder, your resources and finances are incredible; and, hearing you speak many years ago at our church in Franklin, VA was priceless.

To Pastor Bill Winston, I have absorbed your teachings like a sponge. May God continue to prosper your ministry.

To Pastor Creflo, I started watching you in 1998 and my mindset on life and God's abundance has forever been shifted.

To Pastor Mike Pumphrey, you have been a mentor and friend. I am thankful that God allowed our paths to cross.

To Bishop Ronald Molten, I always appreciate your wisdom and words of encouragement. Bless you, Man of God.

To Craig and Chris Turner, I cannot say thank you enough for all that you have done for our family. Thank you for praying me through this project.

To Patricia King, I appreciate your ministry and heart, Woman of God. When I heard you say, "God plus nothing is all you need," it blessed my soul.

Foreword by Apostle James H. Howell

For far too long, the subject of money has been a sensitive topic in the Body of Christ. Even though the Bible says money answereth all things...we're still sensitive...even though it is a vehicle by which we get things accomplished...we're still sensitive...and even though we are avid watchers of television programs whose premise revolves around contestants vying to win the big prize we're still sensitive...and even though we become totally vested in these shows that we become cheerleaders for these contestants in their quest to win "big money".... Yet... We are still sensitive.

I believe that this mindset, this sensitivity, when it comes to money is part of the reason we are not living underneath the open window of blessing promised to us in Malachi, Chapter 3, because although we have become progressive-minded in other areas of ministry like technology, social media, and marketing, our views on money have not advanced as quickly.

The inward cringing and tenseness that happens when we speak about money is an indicator that we have a heart condition, which can only be treated by allowing God to invade those areas of our heart that become dis-eased when we speak of money. It is time for us to allow the Holy Spirit to lead us into all truth so that we can become liberated in our hearts and transformed in our minds regarding matters of finance.

I believe, "Get Off the System: Moving From Lack to Abundance" is a very wonderful prescription that will aid us on our road to recovery. What I love about this book is, not only does it challenge the reader's mind...it also challenges his heart. Pastor Jamison is very forthcoming, scripturally sound and relatable as he presents us with stepping stones to lead us on a path to financial freedom. This book is very timely and significant and belongs in the hands of pastors, church leaders and believers who are ready to take the limits off and live in the overflow.

On a personal note, my relationship with Pastor Jamison spans some 10 plus years and I am honored to call him my son. He is a much sought-after lecturer and preacher who has been consistent in his quest to empower the Body of Christ. I say without reservation that his life is proof that the godly principles detailed in this book, work!!!

Introduction

Lack! Not enough! Struggle! Bills! It's always something! Are these phrases that have proceeded out of your mouth? **Proverbs 3:2** tells us that "you have been trapped by what you said; ensnared by the words of your mouth." If there is one struggle that many people have in common, of all races and all sizes, it is the struggle to break free from financial strain.

Financial challenges and the stress of limited resources have led to divorces, health problems, crimes and a generational cycle of poverty and lack. My own father, who after being laid off from a local chemical plant faced mounting medical bills for my disabled sister. He one day walked up to the counter of a bank and committed armed robbery. Lack, drove him to the only solution his mind could fathom, robbing a bank, which led to a prison sentence. You may not be facing a prison sentence, but are you mentally incarcerated from the inability to escape the land of not enough?

As I wrote in my first book, No More Handcuffs: 5 Keys To Removing The Mental Handcuffs From Your Life, people are often locked up by the circumstances of life. The Bible talks about money more than 2000+ times and more than heaven or hell, still people, especially church folk, cringe when you discuss money and how to stop being a slave to it. In the church world, we have placed ourselves in mental bondage by making it taboo to discuss the one thing people struggle with the most. We can shout about everything in church from God to macaroni and cheese, but when someone discusses money in church, it is the Silence of the Lambs.

Why the resistance? It is because unbeknownst to the church, we truly do not serve God when it comes to our financial resources. We serve mammon or the god of money, instead of making God our source. People reading this may say, "This is blasphemy! Of course, I serve God and not money!" This is what most people think.

Let me propose four questions:

1. Do you get angry, sad and/or anxious when you do not have any money?
2. Do you get worried when you have more bills than money?
3. Do you always think about things you would do if you had more money?
4. Do you always check your bank account to see how much money you have?

If you answered *yes* to any of these questions about God being your source, your heart may not be 100% with God. The text says that one cannot serve both God and mammon. Why? Because you will always show favor to one over the other. When God requires your money for the kingdom, but your heart is with mammon, you will always be led by your emotions instead of by your Spirit.

The Bible reminds us in **Romans 8:2** that "For the law of the Spirit of life in Christ Jesus hath made me free from the law of sin and death." You are either serving God with all your heart and with all your soul and with all your strength and with all your mind, or, you're not! There are no gray areas with God and there are no gray areas when it comes to your money with God.

I love how the Good News translation interprets **Revelation 3:15** by saying, "I know what you have done; I know that you are neither cold nor hot. How I wish you were either one or the other!" As the scripture says, I know what YOU have done. You have allowed "the cares of this life, the deceitfulness of wealth, and the desire for other things come in and choke the word…" **Mark 4:19**.

The conclusion of this book, Get Off The System: Moving From Lack To Abundance, will challenge you to realign yourself with

the Word of God when it comes to your finances. We have seen bad press about preachers and money; the church and money; and all the ills concerning the so-called "Prosperity Theology" and/or "Word of Faith" movement. My goal is to debunk those ills and myths. I intend to press against your intellect to let you know that prosperity through faith, is God's suggestion and not man's.

John 10:10 tells us, "The thief cometh not, but for to steal, and to kill, and to destroy: I am come that they might have life and that they might have it more abundantly." Not only that, the Bible says in **Psalm 35:27**, "Let them shout for joy, and be glad, that favour my righteous cause: yea, let them say continually, Let the LORD be magnified, which hath pleasure in the prosperity of his servant." I think, it is categorically incorrect and biblically immature to say prosperity is a separate theology when it is God's will for us to prosper and be in health, even as our soul prospers.

Get Off The System: Moving From Lack To Abundance will teach you how to break away from the mammon spirit and allow God, your one, and only source to lead you. When God is your source, everything else is just a resource. As Patricia King says, "God plus nothing is all you need."

This is not another book on money or getting rich. It is rather, a rite of passage into God's system of abundance; and, your graduation party from being stuck in the school of lack. God placed these words on my heart to speak to the core of individuals. I understand your hurt; I understand your pain. I understand the stress behind not enough or not having what you need. As God showed me how to get out, I too will show you. A common saying in the African American community is "once we know better, we will do better".

Today, you will learn God's system of how to do better. I am not speaking against employment. I am, however, speaking against anything, including your paycheck, from becoming your source. As you read through these pages, brace yourself! Prepare your mind and allow God's presence and the Holy Spirit to minister to you. May He release the chains from your mind and your pockets so that you can be free. As **John 8:36** tells us, "If the Son, therefore, shall make you free, ye shall be free indeed."

God's Economy

CHAPTER 1

"No man can serve two masters: for either he will hate the one and love the other; or else he will hold to the one and despise the other. Ye cannot serve God and mammon." **Matthew 6:24**

When Jesus breathed this text into existence, He clearly defined two systems that are now, and will forever more be in operation. **Example:** there will always be light and dark, and hot and cold. These systems are tried and true principles, laws, if you will, that will always exist. The same way gravity is a law. It does not matter what your denomination is or how much you give to the church, gravity will still impact you as it impacts everyone else. What are the two systems: God's System and the Mammon System. Mammon is an Aramaic word meaning riches and wealth. It is the spirit behind the money. It is the very thing that causes people to become seduced by its enticements.

Paul explains to Timothy in **1 Timothy 6:9**. "But those who desire to be rich fall into temptation, into a snare, into many senseless and harmful desires that plunge people into ruin and destruction." And then Paul furthers the conversation in verse 10 and says, "For the love of money is the root of all kinds of evil". Someone may ask, "Are you saying that desiring wealth and riches is wrong?" For me to make that statement would be diametrically opposed to the premise of this work. Rather, it is the misplaced desire that is wrong. The mammon system is designed for you to remove your desire from God as your source and place it into something artificial. As the text in 1 Timothy tells us, that when we chase or have misplaced desires for riches, we become trapped and ultimately plunge into a hopeless valley of stress and destruction, all from chasing the wrong thing. The correct desire is for us to seek God's face instead of his hands. To seek the provider more than we seek the provision. To be on our knees instead of always saying, "Will you please?"

The first construct you must understand is how money is the currency that fuels the mammon system. In the mammon system, which our society is built on, we have a 'buy and sell' system. We develop a 'hoarding mentality' or a 'looking out for me and mine' mentality. In the mammon system, the spirit of mammon drives us to pursue overtime on a job, take second and third jobs, and borrow more money just to make ends meet. The truth of the matter is, though, ends never meet. You will stay on the never-ending hamster wheel of life in what is known as the rat race. This is the deceitfulness of riches. In the world's system, they tell you to work 40 years, get a 30-year mortgage, go to college and take out student loans to cover the cost of tuition. I am not speaking against personal development, buying a home and employment, but I am speaking against willingly taking part in a system without knowing that God has something better for you than a time clock or a great job with benefits. I have met people with everything; houses and cars, but they are as empty as the cookie jar at a daycare center. Look at the number of celebrities that commit suicide and get divorced or end up on drugs.

That is why the Bible says in **Mark 8:36**, "For what shall it profit a man, if he shall gain the whole world, and lose his own soul?" Chasing money is the quintessential bait that is cast on the line of life by the spirit of mammon. Unlike the world's system where money is the currency, in God's system, faith is the currency.

The Bible tells us in **Hebrews 11:6**, "But without faith, it is impossible to please him: for he that cometh to God must believe that he is, and that he is a rewarder of them that diligently seek him." In the world's economy, money is viewed as the highest commodity while faith is viewed as the lowest.

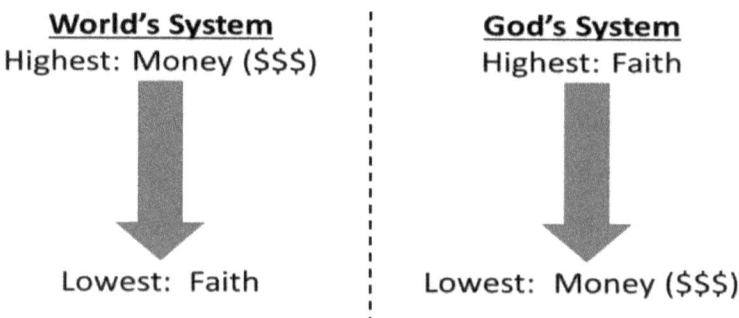

However, in God's system, faith is viewed as the highest commodity while money is regarded as the lowest. So, God is going to use your faith to infiltrate and take over the money in the world's economy and repossess everything that the devil has stolen from you, financially. How do I know the devil is a thief?

John 10:10 tells us that "The thief cometh not, but for to steal, and to kill, and to destroy…" However, the good news can be found in **Proverbs 6:31** concerning the thief when it says, "Yet if caught, he must pay sevenfold; he must give up all the wealth of his house."

So not only are you due sevenfold from what you are missing, but everything in the enemy's house will be transferred to your house. Sounds like a wealth transfer! You are getting everything back, every time you had to pay a co-pay, extra taxes, electric bill, penalties, vehicles that kept breaking down; everything is going to be restored, returned and renewed. When you spend all your money on the previous items, then you have very little left to truly provide for your family or even give to the kingdom of God.

The spirit of mammon has deceived a clear majority of Christians. Mammon will speak to you. Mammon will grip you. Mammon will say, "You do not have to tithe or give." Mammon will remind you of what you cannot afford. Mammon will push you to compare yourself to rich people. Mammon will encourage you to wonder what others do for a living if they have a bigger home or a bigger car than you. Mammon convinces you that debt is the only way to get a car, a house, pay for college or even buy furniture. On the contrary, mammon paints the illusion that I deserve this car that I cannot afford or an outfit that I do not need now. When your nails are done but you do not have gas money, mammon is laughing because it has defeated you again. Mammon is the currency of this world and this world is ruled by Satan.

In **2 Corinthians 4:4** the Bible tells us that, "Satan, who is the god of this world, has blinded the minds of those who do not believe. They are unable to see the glorious light of the Good News. They do not understand this message about the glory of Christ, who is the exact likeness of God."

Mammon enslaves us and produces, as Patricia King called it, a "withholding spirit" in our lives. The withholding spirit will grip us and take over and we will become so tight and fearful of giving anything and will always find a reason not to. Satan has used this withholding spirit to not only blind the minds of those who do not believe in Christ, but he has blinded the minds of Christians who do not realize their citizenship is in heaven and that faith is our currency and not mammon.

Paul was aware of this dynamic in **Philippians 3:20** when he wrote, "But our citizenship is in heaven, and we eagerly await a Savior from there, the Lord Jesus Christ." When someone visits another country, he or she is considered a foreigner and they must have a passport and participate in the foreign exchange process for their currency. Our passport is the Word of God and our exchange is the wealth transfer that God has laid up for us. The Bible tells us in **Proverbs 13:22** that the "wealth of the sinner is laid up for the righteous." If you are wondering who the righteous are, read **2 Corinthians 5:21** where the Word tells us "God made Him who knew no sin to be sin on our behalf so that in Him we might become the righteousness of God."

In layman's terms, Jesus died so that we can become righteous and through our faith in Him we can reclaim everything in this foreign land called earth that belongs to God. **Psalm 24:1** reminds us "The earth is the LORD's and the fullness thereof; the world, and they that dwell therein." Everything belongs to God and the enemy is illegally holding our possessions. Our faith is what is used to make the foreign exchange with mammon or money. We use our faith to take the money from the enemy and bring it back to the kingdom of God. This is the foundation of God's economy. We must take back what has been stolen.

I have been a long-time landlord. In Virginia, when a tenant does not pay their rent, the first step is a five day pay or quit notice. This notifies them that they are late, and they have five days to bring their balance current or prepare to vacate the premises. If they have not paid after five days, you will have to go to the courthouse and pay for a form called an unlawful detainer. An unlawful detainer is a legal form that states someone is unlawfully living in your property. In addition, the unlawful detainer sets a court date with the judge, typically two to three weeks from the date of filing the form. If the person has not moved out by the court date, you will have to go before the judge and show evidence, typically your receipts and the lease, that this person has not paid the rent. Then you must ask the judge for both judgment and possession of your property. After you receive judgment and possession of your property you are legally entitled to take possession of your house again. If the person still has not moved out, you must then go to the sheriff's office and fill out a writ of possession and the sheriff will post a 72-hour notice stating they must leave. If they do not leave after 72 hours, the sheriff will remove them. You will have to change the locks and the sheriff formally gives you possession.

I used this explanation to show you that God, the judge, has given us possession of our property when Jesus died on the cross. You have a legal right to abundance and wealth, but Satan has been living in your property without permission and you are acting as though it is kosher. You must show Him the paperwork, the Word of God, that you have both judgment and possession. If He still refuses to leave then get your other big brother, the Holy Spirit (aka The Sheriff), to let him know he is on notice and you are taking everything back. You do not have to wait 72 hours, you can get your possessions back right now! Stop allowing your economics to be determined by the amount of money you have or do not have. Rather, choose to use a more powerful currency called faith. Remember that we "walk by faith, not by sight" **2 Corinthians 5:7**. It is time to get everything back that belongs to you and walk in the abundance that God has for you in His economy.

God's Abundance

CHAPTER 2

"The thief does not come except to steal, and to kill, and to destroy. I have come that they may have life and that they may have it more abundantly." **John 10:10**

There is no lack in heaven and there should be no lack in your life. Jesus prayed in **Matthew 6:10**, "Your kingdom come. Your will be done on earth as it is in heaven." Since people in heaven are not on food stamps, living paycheck to paycheck or going to title loan places, then why are we? You could argue the mansions in heaven are a form of government housing since God has his own kingdom, but I am ok with that type of government assistance. The challenge for many Christians is that we go to church, give, pray and confess and many of us still struggle to walk in God's abundance. The foundation of walking into God's abundance is understanding the revelation of tithing and giving.

Examine the text in **Genesis 14:17-23**

- ➢ 17 *And the king of Sodom went out to meet him at the Valley of Shaveh (the King's Valley), after his return from the defeat of Chedorlaomer and the kings who were with him.*
- ➢ 18 *Then Melchizedek king of Salem brought out bread and wine; he was the priest of God Most High.*
- ➢ 19 *And he blessed him and said: "Blessed be Abram of God Most High, Possessor of heaven and earth:*
- ➢ 20 *And blessed be God Most High, who has delivered your enemies into your hand." And he gave him a tithe of all.*
- ➢ 21 *Now the king of Sodom said to Abram, "Give me the persons, and take the goods for yourself.*
- ➢ 22 *But Abram said to the king of Sodom, "I have raised my hand to the LORD, God Most High, the Possessor of heaven and earth,*
- ➢ 23 *that I will take nothing, from a thread to a sandal strap, and that I will not take anything that is yours, lest you should say, 'I have made Abram rich.*

We have father Abram and two kings: King of Sodom and the King of Salem. We know Sodom to be a place of defilement, perversion, filth and tied to the world. The Bible describes the King of Salem, Melchizedek, as a priest of the Most-High God. Every time you get your paycheck two kings come to meet you: King of Sodom and the King of Salem. Every time someone gives you money or when you get a refund, etc., you will face these two kings. Elijah even asked the question in **1 Kings 18:21**, "How long will you go limping between two opinions?"

Your abundance is stiffened because you are constantly vacillating between these two kings. Some of you will even say, "I got my tithes out the way or I gave my tithes" as if it is the same as the light bill or phone bill. We must tithe, but we get to give. We essentially received a payday loan from God and every two weeks (or whenever you receive money), we are responsible for paying Him back. We are not doing Him a favor; instead, we are giving Him what is due and constantly reaffirming that we are serving the King of Salem and not the King of Sodom.

James understood this parallel when he said in **James 1:8**, "Their loyalty is divided between God and the world, and they are unstable in everything they do." When your loyalty is divided your abundance will be divided, your wealth will be divided, your increase will be divided, and you will be divided. God, why is it not happening for me? I know I have been giving but I am still struggling? Since Genesis is the book of beginnings, let us look at the beginning.

In **Genesis 2:25** the text says, "And they were both naked, the man and his wife, and were not ashamed." When we are in fellowship with God and withhold nothing from Him, we may seem naked or exposed to the world, but we are spiritually covered. Why? Because the tithes cover us even when we don't think we are covered. Adam and Eve were naked in the natural, but they were not aware of their nakedness because God had them covered spiritually. This spiritual principle is highlighted again in **Matthew 18:18**, "Verily I say unto you, whatsoever ye shall bind on earth shall be bound in heaven: and whatsoever ye shall loose on earth shall be loosed in heaven."

On the contrary, not tithing, is diametrically opposed to God's will and you are resisting His abundance. This is shown after Adam and Eve sinned. The text in **Genesis 3:7** indicates that "the eyes of both were opened, and they knew that they were naked. And they sewed fig leaves together and made themselves loincloths." When we stop tithing and giving, we step out of God's will for His abundance for our lives and now we are spiritually naked but naturally covered. The problem is, we are the ones who are doing the covering. God asked the question in **Genesis 3:11**, "Who told you that you were naked?"

Now, I am asking you the question, "Who told you not to tithe?" When you sometimes give and sometimes withhold, you are taking the Almond Joy approach to God's abundance. Almond Joy, the candy bar, has a slogan that says, "Sometimes you feel like a nut and sometimes you don't." Sometimes you feel like giving and sometimes you don't. That approach to God's abundance will leave you with one leg attached to the King of Sodom and the other leg attached to the King of Salem. Essentially, you are leaving yourself exposed in the middle.

The Bible tells us in **Revelation 3:15-17**

> 15 *I know thy works, that thou art neither cold nor hot: I would thou wert cold or hot.*

> 16 *So then because thou art lukewarm, and neither cold nor hot, I will spew thee out of my mouth.*
> 17 *Because thou sayest, I am rich, and increased with goods, and have need of nothing; and knowest not that thou art wretched, and miserable, and poor, and blind, and naked.*

If God is not God of all, then He is not God at all, in your life. Unfortunately, many of us, including myself, have found this out the hard way. To walk in God's abundance and experience it on this side of heaven, especially in the financial realm, you must treat God as your only source and not just a resource. David understood this principle when he wrote in **Psalm 27:13**, "I am certain that I will see the LORD's goodness in the land of the living." David understood that regardless of how hard it gets, I am still trusting in the only one that can help me and deliver me.

As modern-day Christ-followers, we often refer to **Galatians 3:29**, "And if ye be Christ's, then are ye Abraham's seed, and heirs according to the promise." If this is the case, we cannot overlook that Abraham gave tithes to Melchizedek, who was his High Priest. Abraham tithed long before the law. I like what the Bible says in **Hebrews 5:10** "and He was declared by God a high priest in the order of Melchizedek." If I can digress for a moment and highlight the revelation that some of us may be missing.

Here in **Hebrews 5:10** Jesus is being called a High Priest. In the Old Testament and throughout scripture there was a line drawn between the king and priest. The king ruled, and the priest kept the sacraments. Now, through Jesus, we have a Priest that used himself as the Lamb for sacrifice and we have a King that came to rule. This powerful marriage provides clarity and insight as to why the Word says in **Revelation 1:6**, "And hath made us kings and priests unto God and his Father; to him be glory and dominion forever and ever. Amen." Why is this important and how does it relate to your abundance?

Jesus has sole authority and final say over the abundance in your life. He is both king and priest. Your abundance is not determined by your employer's pay raise, a better job or hitting the lottery (which you shouldn't be playing anyway). It is through Christ alone. The Word affirms this truth in **Psalm 75:6-7**, "For promotion cometh neither from the east, nor from the west, nor from the south. But God is the judge: he putteth down one, and setteth up another." That is powerful because I do not have to chase the world and the things of the world. Instead, I can chase the Man with the plan and that Man is Jesus. The same way Melchizedek gave Abraham the blessing is the same way Jesus will bless us in exchange for our tithes.

Tithing is not about the money, even though it is hard for people to grasp that notion. God does not need your money, nor is heaven selling chicken dinners to pay for the streets of gold. Rather, God is after your heart. The tithe, in the natural, is used to fund and build the ministry that you are sowing into. What if they misuse my money? The question I ask is this, "Is it really your money?" If we owe someone $20, when we give it back we never say, "I hope they do not waste it." We do not say that because it does not belong to us.

If the tithe does not belong to you, then when you give it, it does not matter if the church misuses it or not, because it was never yours in the first place. It is your obligation to do your part which is to return it back to God and your blessing comes not from the pastor, but from God. If they misuse it, they will have to give an account and suffer the consequences both naturally and spiritually, but your prosperity will not be affected by their mismanagement or lack of stewardship.

I've been married over 15 years and one thing I learned in marriage is that everything hinges on proper communication. It is often not what you say but how you say it that truly matters. Tithing is the same way. It is not what you give (in term of what dollar value your 10% is) but how you give it that matters. Are you giving the 10 percent out of complete trust in God as your source or are you giving it and watching it travel down the aisle in the offering bucket? God is trying to take you off the system of trusting in mammon and bring you over into His system which is a more excellent way. While on the conversation of 10 percent, let us dispel the myth or confusion of what we should give in our tithe.

Merriam-Webster refers to the tithe as follows:

- a tenth part of something paid as a voluntary contribution or as a tax especially for the support of a religious establishment
- the obligation represented by individual tithes
- a small part
- a small tax or levy

The Bible tells us in **Hebrews 7:1-2**

> 1 *For this Melchizedek, king of Salem, priest of the Most-High God, who met Abraham returning from the slaughter of the kings and blessed him.*
> 2 *To whom also Abraham gave a tenth part of all; first being by interpretation King of righteousness, and after that also King of Salem, which is, King of peace."*

Abraham gave a tenth of all. He did not give a tenth of his net but of his gross. He did not give a tenth of what was left after Uncle Sam bit off the top. The tithe is a tenth of that first number at the top of your paycheck, not the net (after everything has been deducted). As Author and Speaker Ray Linder says, "Do you want God to bless you off of your net or your gross." As Ray mentioned, we are essentially trying to figure out how to give the least amount of money to God and still get His maximum blessing!

As I discuss this topic with you, my heart is not to convict or to condemn, but rather bring clarity and revelation about tithing. This is truly a heart issue. I have seen devout Christians trust God for all types of healing, job opportunities, for doors to open and still they struggle financially. So, I asked God two questions. The first question is, "Why some Christians who have been tithing for years are still broke?" If you have been giving, then you should not be as broke as the Ten Commandments Moses dropped at Mount Sinai.

The Lord led me to **Matthew 6:7** where it says, "But when ye pray, use not vain repetitions, as the heathen do: for they think that they shall be heard for their much speaking." I thought to myself, 'this is an interesting scripture about tithing'. Then I realized what God was showing me. The same way the heathens pray using vain repetitions, people give their tithes with vain repetition. The same way these meaningless repetitions are used by the heathens in prayer, the same way we are tithing with no meaning. The motive behind tithing should not be because we don't want the pastor to talk about us, or we do not want to go to hell or be plagued with a curse. We have developed a mundane routine of giving our tithes out of habit instead of out of love and adoration for God our Father and Provider. Tithing is no longer sacred and significant, but just something else we do on Sundays.

It's like when you have been in a relationship with someone for a while and you start taking things for granted and forget the reason why you were put together in the first place. Tithing is more than placing a check in the offering bucket and claiming your blessing. **Matthew 6:8 says**, "Be not ye, therefore, like unto them: for your Father knoweth what things ye have need of, before ye ask him." God knows what you need before you write the check, so the tithe even though it biblical guarantees God's blessing, is not the root of why God blesses us. God blesses us because He is a Good Father. He blesses us just because we are his children. The Bible says in **1 Peter 2:9**, "But you are a chosen people, a royal priesthood, a holy nation, God's special possession, that you may declare the praises of him who called you out of darkness into his wonderful light."

His blessing is the ability to prosper in everything that we do. The blessing is not necessarily the new Cadillac or house, rather, it is the ability to get and do whatever we need. It is His super on our natural, giving us the supernatural ability to do more than we can ever imagine. Do not allow routine to diminish the sacred work of the tithing exchange. The same way communion is still sacred every time we take it, you must treat tithing in the same manner.

The second question that I asked God is, "What if someone wants to tithe but they have bills due today and they feel like they cannot tithe?" The Lord led me to two passages of scriptures in response to this question. The first scripture is in **Psalm 118:5-8**. "I called to the LORD in distress; the LORD answered me and put me in a spacious place." When you are bound in this situation, you should have one prayer, "Lord, make space for me." That is powerful, God make space for me! If the world makes space for you, they can take it back because the world is based on a crooked and corrupt system. But when God makes space for you, then we will walk into the fullness of **Revelation 3:8** "I know thy works: behold, I have set before thee an open door, and no man can shut it: for thou hast a little strength, and hast kept my word, and hast not denied my name."

The second scripture that God led me to is **1 Chronicles 4:10**: "Jabez called on the God of Israel, saying, Oh that thou wouldest bless me indeed, and enlarge my coast, and that thine hand might be with me, and that thou wouldest keep me from evil, that it may not grieve me! And God granted him that which he requested." When Jabez said enlarge my coast or territory, he was pleading with God to make space for Him. Jabez was born into a rough situation, but after God heard his cry in distress, He made space for him. Are you in distress financially? Do you need God to make space for you? Do you need some doors opened that no one can shut?

Then cry out to God right now and read this prayer out loud:

Father, please forgive me for putting my trust in mammon instead of putting my trust in You. I repent for not making You my one and only source. Please hear my cry as I come to You". The Bible says in **John 14:14**, "If I ask anything in Your name, You will do it." I understand that I have a blood-bought right through Christ to boldly come to Your throne. I come to You in the name of Jesus asking You to make space for me. Rebuke the devourer out of my life and restore the years the locust has eaten. I will honor You with my tithe in my heart and in my deed and I will seek You first and not lean to my own understanding. I now command the blessing of God to overtake my life and overtake my finances and I will forever live in overflow. In Jesus name, Amen".

God's Entrepreneur

CHAPTER 3

"And God said, Let us make man in our image, after our likeness: and let them have dominion over the fish of the sea, and over the fowl of the air, and over the cattle, and over all the earth, and over every creeping thing that creepeth upon the earth." **Genesis 1:26**

When God made us, He created us to be another speaking spirit. We were created in His image to be dual dominators. That is why He made us both kings and priests because He wants us to dominate in the ministry and the marketplace. Everyone cannot work for the church. We need Christian: engineers, lawyers, doctors, accountants, welders, mechanics, and we need Christian politicians. We need to represent Christ in everything. When we have ownership, we can dictate what the world does instead of the world dictating our course of action. If we owned a hotel, we can choose to not allow adult movies to be shown in our hotel rooms. If we owned a strip mall we could determine which businesses to allow instead of a business that may hurt the community. Everyone has the seed of entrepreneurship planted on the inside of them from creation. Entrepreneurs create something from nothing. God created us from nothing (or the dirt). We do not have to depend on the world's system to be our crutch when God has designed us to walk on our own in Him. God didn't design you to be in government housing or to use EBT cards. God didn't design you to depend on a paycheck or wait on Friday or for your tax refund.

David said in **1 Samuel 17: 36-37**, "Thy servant slew both the lion and the bear: and this uncircumcised Philistine shall be as one of them, seeing he hath defied the armies of the living God. David said moreover, The LORD that delivered me out of the paw of the lion, and out of the paw of the bear, he will deliver me out of the hand of this Philistine. And Saul said unto David, Go, and the LORD be with thee."

You have overcome so much in your life, so you must treat lack and not enough the same way David treated Goliath. David knew, today, he was going to overcome this Giant and overcome this obstacle and remove fear out of the lives of His people because of Goliath. Are you ready to remove the obstacle of not enough and remove the fear of lack from your own family?

I loved what the Lord tells Joshua in **Joshua 11:6**, "And the LORD said unto Joshua, be not afraid because of them: for tomorrow about this time will I deliver them up all slain before Israel: thou shalt hough their horses and burn their chariots with fire." Tomorrow about this time! What a powerful statement from the Lord. Put this statement in your own context. Tomorrow about this time you will be a millionaire! You will be healed! You will get a promotion…. tomorrow about this time!

Do not discount what the Lord can do in one day because in **2 Kings 7:1**, Elisha says, "Listen to this message from the LORD! This is what the LORD says: By this time tomorrow in the markets of Samaria, five quarts of choice flour will cost only one piece of silver, and ten quarts of barley grain will cost only one piece of silver." In the words of Pastor Bill Winston, there is going to be plenty and it is going to be cheap. Do not discount what God can do in one day. Creation was done in six days. In one day, the children of Israel crossed the Red Sea and escaped hundreds of years of bondage. On the third day, our Savior Jesus Christ rose with all power in his hand.

The Bible reminds us in **2 Peter 3:8-9**, But, beloved, be not ignorant of this one thing, that one day is with the Lord as a thousand years and a thousand years as one day. The Lord is not slack concerning his promise, as some men count slackness; but is longsuffering to us-ward, not willing that any should perish, but that all should come to repentance.

So why is understanding all these concepts fundamental to becoming God's entrepreneur? Many entrepreneurs, especially those who become successful, often say they are "self-made millionaires". I submit to you that we are God-made and not of ourselves. In God's system, time is not a factor as it is in the world's system for God's entrepreneurs. Jesus recognized this in the New Testament because the first people He called were already entrepreneurs.

He said in **Matthew 4:19**, "And he saith unto them, follow me, and I will make you fishers of men." Jesus knew that if they understood how something worked in the world's system then He could use the same concept to teach them how to operate in His system. Then He begins to show them that when you do things God's way you can move faster than the world's way.

I am reminded of the miracle in John 2 of how Jesus turned the water into wine and how it went against common sense and logic. This should be encouraging, not for a license to drink, but to know that if Jesus wants us to have something then He will provide it. For where there is vision, there is also provision. In making wine mentioned by Laurel Gray Vineyards, first, there is a harvesting process where the grapes are picked. Then there is a crushing and pressing process for the grapes. Then there is a fermentation process which can take up to a month. Then there is a clarification process where dead cells and other items are removed. Then you get to the final process of aging and bottling. So, Jesus went from water, which is not even grapes, to the aging and bottling process, circumventing both time and scientific reasoning.

This is how we operate as a God-driven entrepreneur. We operate with the kingdom as our guide and walk with a constant expectation of the supernatural in our work. Miracles happen because they override time. If you break your arm, it will take six to eight weeks to heal, but supernatural healing can happen in six to eight seconds. Beyond having a job, God has designed you to always have multiple streams of income flowing into your household. One man said that your salary on your job is what they pay you to postpone your dream. I have always been a believer in the concept that if your name is not on the building then you are building someone else's dream.

In **Genesis, 2:10-15**

- ➢ 10 And a river went out of Eden to water the garden; and from thence it was parted and became into four heads.
- ➢ 11 The name of the first is Pison: that is it which compasseth the whole land of Havilah, where there is gold;
- ➢ 12 And the gold of that land is good: there is bdellium and the onyx stone.
- ➢ 13 And the name of the second river is Gihon: the same is it that compasseth the whole land of Ethiopia.
- ➢ 14 And the name of the third river is Hiddekel: that is it which goeth toward the east of Assyria. And the fourth river is Euphrates.
- ➢ 15 And the LORD God took the man and put him into the Garden of Eden to dress it and to keep it.

When you begin to dig deeper, you will find the significance of these four rivers in their meaning. Pison is said to mean fruitful, all-encompassing and full of riches. Gihon is said to mean a gushing fountain or bursting forth. Hiddekel means the rapid Tigris or Great River. Euphrates means sweet water, good and abounding. When applying these definitions to your own life, God wants every Christian to have at least four streams of income that are flowing into your life. The streams should all be fruitful, full of riches, all-encompassing to the point that increase is bursting forth at a rapid pace leaving you in a sweet, good and abounding place. Wow! God is so much wiser than we are. Even in the book of beginnings as He prepared to give Adam his assignment to work in the garden, He already provided four streams to help him with his work.

God wants to help you with your work. When you live by your paycheck, you will never have enough. Why? Because it was never designed that way. God made those streams first, even before He gave Adam a job. You can own multiple businesses and not even have a job! Often, a job or J.O.B is just over broke! In the world's system you punch a clock and get lost in the competition of the rat race but in God's system, you create what you do not have. I am not against jobs, I am against working for someone else your whole life and never realizing that God wants you to have money flowing into your life from multiple directions.

You may be wondering what the purpose is, of having additional income coming into your life. First and foremost, why would more money be a problem? Most of you have a checkbook issue more than any other issue. But to be in sync with the Word, turn your attention to **Exodus 25:1-8** after the children of Israel left Egypt:

- ➢ 1 And the LORD spake unto Moses, saying,
- ➢ 2 Speak unto the children of Israel, that they bring me an offering: of every man that giveth it willingly with his heart ye shall take my offering.
- ➢ 3 And this is the offering which ye shall take of them; gold, and silver, and brass,

- ➢ 4 And blue, and purple, and scarlet, and fine linen, and goats' hair,
- ➢ 5 And rams' skins dyed red, and badgers' skins, and shittim wood,
- ➢ 6 Oil for the light, spices for anointing oil, and for sweet incense,
- ➢ 7 Onyx stones, and stones to be set in the ephod, and in the breastplate.
- ➢ 8 And let them make me a sanctuary; that I may dwell among them.

Verse 8 gives you the purpose of money for the believer. We are to use our financial resources, primarily, to build the kingdom of God or a place where God can dwell. Secondly, if the children of Israel were still poor after leaving Egypt then how could they provide this offering? God brought them out with wealth and abundance.

How does verse 8 look in the natural? Taking care of your man/woman of God so they can focus on leading the ministry and hearing from God instead of worrying about paying their own bills is one example. Another example is when the church can pay for additions to the church in cash instead of financing the project. Or, when the ministry can feed people in the community or renovate someone's home and pay for it in cash, instead of having to raise an offering or selling chicken dinners. Another example is when the ministry can cover the cost of TV or radio time without having to beg for financial help every month from viewers and listeners. The Bible tells us in **Luke 10:27** to "love the Lord your God with all your heart and with all your soul and with all your strength and with all your mind, and your neighbor as yourself." Our strength is more than our biceps, it is our resources. When God blesses you, He does not rain down cars, money, and houses from heaven; instead, He comes in a small still voice and speaks ideas and witty inventions into your spirit. Since you are created to be another speaking spirit, you must speak those things into existence.

The Bible reminds us in **Romans 4:17** to "calleth those things which are not, as though they were." You are then called to take the vision and write it down and start developing a plan. As the Lord tells Habakkuk to "Write the vision, and make it plain upon tables, that he may run that readeth it" **Habakkuk 2:2**. When those ideas come, they are not suggestions; rather, it is God's way of creating a stream in your life. From selling banana pudding to flipping houses, God pours ideas into you daily. No idea that God speaks to you is a stupid idea. When you ask for financial help, He gives you ideas that will help create space for you. Trust Him and lean not unto your own understanding and He will direct your path.

Learn how to create God-centered goals within your business that your business may grow and flourish. Goals are nothing more than dreams with a deadline. Learn how to set both short, intermediate and long-term goals and work on your plan like your life depends on it because it does. You must want to fulfill your purpose as a God-driven entrepreneur as badly as you do your next breath. One of the key concepts in becoming an entrepreneur is understanding the Growth Cycle of becoming an entrepreneur.

Examine the chart:

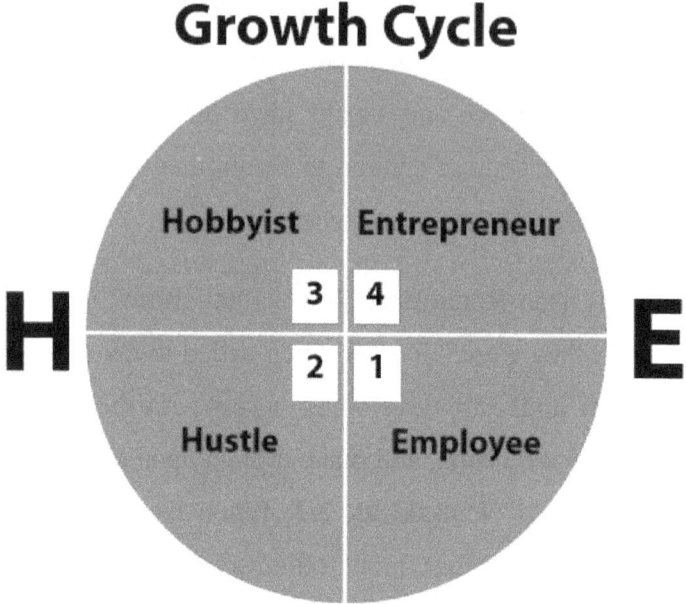

The first category for most people is *an employee*. An employee works for someone else and their primary function is to fill a role in the company and to be an asset to someone else's business. Being an employee has tremendous value because it teaches you a lot about your strengths and weaknesses and what it takes for businesses to be successful. I still remember the lessons I learned from my first job at McDonald's.

The second category is *the hustler*. A hustler is someone that sells anything (legal) that will make them extra cash. This could range from chicken dinners to cutting hair on the side. The Hustler is concerned about making extra money to help with their current obligations. Hustlers just want to get ahead.

The third category in the progression is *the hobbyist*. The hobbyist has graduated from being a "jack of all trades" to becoming more focused on one or two specific ideas instead of being all over the place. The hobbyist has realized what he or she is good at (or is selling the most of) and decides to take it more seriously. In the hobbyist category, I also include people who are self-employed (ex. Real Estate Agent, Plumber, Motivational Speaker, etc.). This person has learned how to generate an income based on their gifts and passions, however; it still requires them to be present and continuously active in the day-to-day operations of their business for it to be successful. The business often rises and falls on their output.

The fourth category is *the entrepreneur*. This is the category that we all should strive to reach. As an entrepreneur you are still actively involved in your business, but you have other people (employees), not just an assistant, who are building your business. You are providing quality jobs for others and you can operate at more of 30K foot level instead of getting lost in the "daily grind." This is the growth cycle that we must go through to become successful entrepreneurs. As an entrepreneur you will not only grow your business, you will constantly find new ways to grow additional streams of income. The best entrepreneurs are the people who hire and train people to have an entrepreneur mindset, even as an employee.

As you work on growing your streams, follow my 7 rules of creating multiple streams of income.

1. Build one stream at a time
2. Properly manage your stream
3. Become X-Stream
4. Turn your stream into a mighty river
5. Tell everyone about your stream
6. Create more stream
7. Enjoy the view

Rule #1 Building one stream at a time requires you to become a student of your craft to become successful. You must read and absorb everything you can about your business. Readers are leaders. In addition, you must tap into larger bodies of water. Simply put, you must network with other successful entrepreneurs, both locally and nationwide. Just because you are a Christian, it does not exempt you from doing the basic things that all entrepreneurs do and that is network. Being a Christian entrepreneur means that our profits are determined by God and not solely on our own efforts. Next, you must find a fisherman to teach you how to fish. You must find mentors to help you along your entrepreneur path. It has been said that if you take the average income of your five closest friends around you that amount normally equals your income. If you want to change your net worth, then you must change your network. You must find people who are better than you to grow your business. You must develop the stream mindset. You must develop the mindset that money is a stream and not a pool. A pool is stagnant. So, if you feel like your money is not moving or growing it is because you are stagnant, and you have the wrong mindset.

Rule #2 To properly manage the stream you must set up banks around the stream. You must set boundaries around your income stream to protect it. Make sure you have the proper tools to track the income (ex. business software, accountant, business budget). In addition, you must monitor flow and look out for waterfalls. You cannot spend everything that you make. You need to set aside 25% to 30% to account for taxes, emergencies, and new opportunities. You must stay at the waterfront. This means that you should stay involved in your business. You must inspect what you expect daily. It does not mean that you cannot delegate and hire employees, but it means you should always be aware of what is going on in your "kitchen." The last aspect of Rule 2 is to stay away from lifeguards. This sounds funny, but it means people who are keeping you from making progress. Some people are always trying to hold you back and restrain you from what God has for you.

Rule #3 Become X-Stream by looking to fill dry places. Your business and ministry, as well, should look to fill a need in the marketplace. You need to keep the stream flowing in the right direction. You always want to make sure that you are operating at a profit. Whenever you are losing money, you need to adjust quickly. Do not become a pool. A pool is stationary and does not grow. Your business must constantly grow and evolve to stay sharp and to stay on top. Yes, we have competitors, but we also have a creator mindset; not a competitor mindset. As Christian entrepreneurs, we are in a league of our own. Lastly, you need to find out where the larger streams are flowing. Keep an eye on your competition and those who are successful at what you are doing. Your competition will give you insight into changes in your industry. In addition, spending time with God will give you revelation on where to take your business next.

Rule #4 Turn your stream into a mighty river. Begin by creating daily lookout points. You must have a systematic way to monitor your business daily. Create a system to handle floods and droughts. A business has ebbs and flows and you do not want to constantly go from feast to famine as an entrepreneur. Learn how to swim. In other words, make sure you know how everything works and functions in your business. It does not mean you do everything, but it means you understand how it works. Finally, protect your stream. Have proper insurance, licenses and even legal protection. It is critical to your success.

Rule #5 Tell everyone about your stream. Don't just exist as another business in a world of businesses but become the first and only choice in your area. What are you doing to separate yourself? Discover why people use your stream. Your customers are your biggest asset. Discover why they buy from you or use your business and design services to meet their needs. Ask your customers for feedback. Do not beat yourself over the head, just ask them for their input. Feedback can be a gift if received in the right spirit and you learn how to make the necessary changes as a result. Adjust, but never stop flowing. Even when you make changes in your business, always keep moving forward.

Rule #6 Create more streams to grow the empire that God is creating for you. Remember all this additional wealth is used first and foremost to build the kingdom of God and to take you off the system of borrowing and living overextended because now you will have enough resources to pay in cash. More streams mean more options. As an entrepreneur, you want to own multiple businesses to help create jobs for more people. Don't limit yourself to just one business. Allow God to birth all your ideas so that you won't die empty because you put everything He gave you into motion. Teach other people to watch your streams. It is your job to work *on* your business, but not *in* your business. As your business grows, teach other people how to manage the day-to-day tasks of your business. I have always been a fan of using virtual assistants to grow my own businesses. These are individuals who can work from home anywhere in the country and can manage multiple tasks in your business virtually. Everything from making calls, mailing leaders, and preparing documents. Virtual assistants can help to make your life easier. You can search for virtual assistants on the internet and you will find more than enough information about this topic. Do not get attached to one stream!

Even the brook dried up for Elijah in **1 Kings 17:7**. Some businesses do not last forever. The demand for them may decrease over time. Always be on the lookout for other streams. Pay close attention to other businesses that you can acquire or get involved with.

Rule #7 Learn how to enjoy the view. Don't forget to go fishing! Take time to enjoy your success. All work and no play make Jack a dull boy. Teach your kids how to fish. As an entrepreneur, it is your duty to teach others, especially your children, to think and act like an entrepreneur. One concept that I want to drill into you is that bait does not matter when you own the river. It does not matter if you have competition if you are leading the pack. Focus on staying ahead and keeping God first so you can stay ahead. Lastly, do not drown in your own prosperity. Remember it is not all about the money. Don't forget how you got there and the people that has helped you, including God. Be encouraged as you become God's entrepreneur. Remember, you are God-made; never self-made!

God's Labor

CHAPTER 4

Hebrews 4:9-12

- 9 There remaineth therefore a rest to the people of God.
- 10 For he that is entered into his rest, he also hath ceased from his own works, as God did from his.
- 11 Let us labour, therefore, to enter into that rest, lest any man fall after the same example of unbelief.
- 12 For the word of God is quick, and powerful, and sharper than any two-edged sword, piercing even to the dividing asunder of soul and spirit, and of the joints and marrow, and is a discerner of the thoughts and intents of the heart."

I remember when I went through a period where I had constant shortness of breath and chest pains. I went to my allergist and my allergist sent me to an ear, nose and throat doctor. My ear, nose and throat doctor sent me to a pulmonologist. The pulmonologist sent me to a cardiologist. The cardiologist put me on a treadmill at different speeds and did a stress test. Then the cardiologist sent the results back to my pulmonologist. After having a follow-up meeting with my pulmonologist, he looked at all my results and said, "You are perfectly fine." I said, but what about the pain I am still experiencing? He said two words that I will never forget, "Push Through".

I submit to you that when it comes to overcoming stress, anxiety, fear and worry, you must push through. Stress keeps us paying co-pays, on medication, having surgeries and missing out on life. Even though church folk despises when the pastor discusses money, most of them are struggling with some type of financial issue. If people can get rid of this financial stronghold of not enough they will be amazed at how their quality of life will immediately improve. There are very few stressor's like financial stress. Outside of a serious or terminal illness, very few things can compare to the weight of not having enough. Because of not having enough, people get two and three jobs, fight for more overtime and are always looking for the latest network marketing business to sign up for.

The text in Hebrews is powerful because it first reveals to us that God has prepared a rest for us. Jesus leaves us some final parting words in **John 14:27** when he says, "Peace I leave with you, my peace I give unto you: not as the world giveth, give I unto you. Let not your heart be troubled, neither let it be afraid." You may wonder what rest has to do with getting off the system. The short answer is, everything. Switching from the mammon system to the faith system requires us to rest in God's presence and allow our lives to rest in His life. Because you may give, and it will look as if you have less money or it may feel like your harvest is taking forever. Or, the moment you sow a financial seed, your check engine light comes on in your car on or the HVAC unit goes out at your house. The only way you can make it through is by resting in Him. Jesus, even in these parting words, clearly defines two systems in constant operating. That is why He said my peace is of a different system than the world's peace. The world's peace is gained by buying something that makes you feel good like a bigger car or house. God's peace, however, comes from the inside out. You can live in a one-bedroom apartment, your bills are all paid, and you somehow feel peaceful and happy as an ant in a bowl of sugar.

When we seek the world's peace we end up chasing more stuff to fill a void that only God can fill. If Jesus warns us to not let our hearts be troubled nor be anxious or afraid, then you can believe things will come to attack your heart. The thief comes to steal, kill and destroy and one of the main things he is after is your peace. Not having peace means that you are afraid that God's Word may not work or may not work quickly enough. Not having peace moves you into the realm of comparing yourself to others and even into self-righteousness where you begin to say, "I know I go to church more than them, but God is blessing them more than me?" But there is a place called rest prepared by God for us. There is something special when God prepares a place for you.

In **Exodus 33:21** God tells Moses that "there is a place by me where you shall stand on the rock." Jesus said in **John 14:3**, "And if I go and prepare a place for you, I will come again, and receive you unto myself; that where I am, there ye may be also." God has a place prepared for you, so you can find rest. Now, in **Hebrews 4:11** it discusses how our only job or labor is to enter into His rest. Before the fall of man, Adam's only job was to till the land, but after the fall he had to labor and work and toil.

1 Corinthians 15:45 shows us that, "The first man, Adam, became a living person." But the last — Adam that is, Christ is — a life-giving Spirit." Jesus became the second Adam and the same thorns and thistles that Adam toiled, Jesus put the crown of thorns and thistles on his head and took all our laboring, stress, working 10 jobs to the cross. Now our only job is rest.

Luke 5:3-4 says…

- 3 And he entered into one of the ships, which was
- Simon's, and prayed him that he would thrust out a little from the land. And he sat down and taught the people out of the ship.
- 4 Now when he had left speaking, he said unto Simon, launch out into the deep, and let down your nets for a draught." When we rest in God, He will take what is not working in our lives, first give us rest, then He will give us instruction. His instruction will take us further than we have been before. You cannot launch out into the deep until you learn how to rest in Him.

Psalm 127:2 reminds us that, "In vain you rise early and stay up late, toiling for food to eat — for he grants sleep to those he loves." What is sleep, sleep is rest? What is rest, is it more sleep? It is much more than that. It is when your cares and anxieties are laid at the cross and you leave them there. I saw an illustration of a pastor giving a watch to someone in the church. The watch represented all our cares and troubles. After the pastor gave it to the individual he kept trying to look at the watch from afar and wondered how it was doing. This is exactly what we do to God. We cast our cares on Him but then we keep worrying about the cares that we should no longer have. You see, when you work, God does not! When God works, then, you can rest.

The Bible tells us in **Psalm 121:4** that God does not "sleep or slumber" so why should we be up all night. The Psalmist said in **Psalm 55:6**, "Oh, that I had the wings of a dove! I would fly away and be at rest." My own personal prayer has been patterned after **Psalm 34:4**, "I sought the LORD, and he answered me; he delivered me from all my fears." Learning how to cast our cares on God and leave them there is one of the greatest challenges of life. How can we learn how to have sparrow faith?

Jesus said in **Matthew 6:25-28**

- 25 Therefore I tell you, do not be anxious about your life, what you will eat or what you will drink, nor about your body, what you will put on. Is not life more than food, and the body more than clothing?
- 26 Look at the birds of the air: they neither sow nor reap nor gather into barns, and yet your heavenly Father feeds them. Are you not of more value than they?
- 27 And which of you by being anxious can add a single hour to his span of life?
- 28 And why are you anxious about clothing?"

Sparrow faith, like the birds, is when you realize that God is going to provide for me just because He is a Good Father, so I am going to leave tomorrow up to Him and enjoy today. **Write this down!** Stress robs you, but rest restores you. God is in the restoration business. **Joel 2:25** tell us that "And I will restore to you the years that the locust hath eaten, the cankerworm, and the caterpillar, and the palmerworm, my great army which I sent among you."

God is in the rest and restoration business. Why is it so hard to be at peace? It is because worry and anxiety are the glue that keeps the world's system together. We have often been raised in the world's system with a worldly mindset trying to live a godly life. It's hard to go from caring to give all your cares to a man named Jesus whom you cannot see, but your cares you can still see. Therefore, Jesus said in **Matthew 11:28-29**

- ➢ 28 Come unto me, all ye that labour and are heavy laden, and I will give you rest.
- ➢ 29 Take my yoke upon you and learn of me; for I am meek and lowly in heart: and ye shall find rest unto your souls."

Our spirits do not need rest. The Bible reminds us in **Hebrews 12:23**, "to the general assembly and church of the firstborn who are enrolled in heaven, and to God, the Judge of all, and to the spirits of the righteous made perfect." Our spirits are perfect through Christ, but our soul which is composed of our mind, will, and intellect, is where we struggle. That is why the Word divides the soul and spirit to identify the root of our issue. Jesus is offering us rest and peace in Him so that your mind can be at rest. The moment you enter His rest, the rest (pun intended) is history. You will begin to experience the fullness of His love.

Now we can grasp **1 John 4:18** when it states, "There is no fear in love, but perfect love casts out fear: because fear hath torment. He that feareth is not made perfect in love." When we are not in rest, we are not made perfect through the love of God. When we enter His rest, we are now in His perfect love and there is nothing that we fear. I will be the first to admit that as a man, especially as an African American man in this society, it is often hard to enter His rest. From the pressure of providing for your family, the social tension of being an African American male, to the weight of the ministry. It is often tough to find peace. But, God has taught me that "The LORD will perfect that which concerns me **Psalm 138:8**.

God also reminded me that He "always causeth us to triumph in Christ, and maketh manifest the savour of his knowledge by us in every place." You must understand what rest is and what it means. Rest is allowing God to ease your mind and give you insight and revelation on the situations in your life. Rest does not mean that the issues no longer exist, it means that the issues are no longer wrapped around you like a blanket but are at the feet of Jesus. Yes, it may be due today, or you need it by Friday, but your situation does not cause heaven to hyperventilate.

God is moved by our faith and rest requires you to activate your faith. The reason we do not rest is because internally and subconsciously, mammon is our source and not God. I know you do not want to admit that. Why do you get excited when you have enough money to do what you need to do, but depressed when the money is low? How can money control your emotions? I will tell you how, because you are attached to it like a tick is attached to a dog, not realizing that it is sucking the life out of you. You must seek rest like your life depends on it, and for some of us, it truly does.

That is why Jesus said in **Mark 2:27** that, "The Sabbath was made for man, and not man for the Sabbath." God even designed a day for us to rest and we still do not rest. Yes, we live out **Lamentations 5:5** when it says, "Our pursuers are at our necks; we are worn out, there is no rest for us." Are your creditors at your neck? Are the cares of life covering you like a blanket? I am here to repeat the instructions left by Paul in **Philippians 4:6-7** 6 Do not be anxious about anything, but in everything by prayer and supplication with thanksgiving let your requests be made known to God.

> 7 And the peace of God, which surpasses all understanding, will guard your hearts and your minds in Christ Jesus."

To find rest, our minds must be washed and renewed with the Word of God. **Romans 12:2** says, "And be not conformed to this world: but be ye transformed by the renewing of your mind, that ye may prove what is that good, and acceptable, and perfect, will of God." When our minds are washed with the water of the Word then we can begin to shift our thinking. See when our gas tank is on E, we fear running out of gas. So, we go to the gas station, fill up our tank and immediately the fear is gone. With the Word of God, you have 66 filling stations you can fill up on daily. I have noticed when my prayer life is low, and my reading time had decreased then I can easily slip into worry and feel anxious. That is why **Psalm 16:8** says,

"I have set the LORD continually before me; Because He is at my right hand, I will not be shaken."

We must, according to **Psalm 34:14**, seek peace and pursue it. What are you in pursuit of? More stuff or more God? We must hunger and thirst after righteousness and be in relentless pursuit of God. We must get to a place that Paul mentions in **Philippians 2:5**, where he says, "Let this mind be in you, which was also in Christ Jesus." When we have the mind of Christ, we can rest. We cannot have the mind of Christ when we do not seek Him and go after him. Yes, we will always have problems in this world. Paul reminds Timothy in **2 Timothy 3:12**, "Yea, and all that will live godly in Christ Jesus shall suffer persecution. **1 Peter 5:7**, says to, "Cast all your anxiety on Him, because He cares for you."

God cares for you. He wants to carry what you are carrying. The same way hell wasn't designed for people, cares were not designed for people to carry. My kids do not have any cares. When they need something, they let me know and move on with their life. Why? Because I'm a good father and they have complete trust in me that I will meet their needs. But how much better is our heavenly father, who is the ultimate father and provider? Often, when we have broken relationships with our own parents, we struggle to have an intimate relationship with our heavenly father. The foundation of rest is trusting in God's Word unconditionally. God is waiting for you to return to Him and give Him all your cares, the same way the father was waiting in anticipation for the prodigal son. As you meditate on learning how to rest, ask God to reveal to you the cares you are carrying. It will take resting in Him to completely transition from the world to God's system. As you rest, meditate on the names of God and our Savior Jesus Christ.

NAMES	SCRIPTURE
Holy One	Mark 1:24
Emmanuel	Matthew 1:23
Rose of Sharon, Lily of the Valley	Song of Solomon 2:1
Lamb of God	John 1:29
King of Kings, and Lord of Lords	Revelation 19:16
I AM	John 8:58
The Way, The Truth, and The Life	John 14:6
Messiah	John 1:41
Savior	II Peter 2:20
Author and Finisher of Our Faith	Hebrews 12:2
Chief Shepherd	I Peter 5:4
Word of Life	I John 1:1
Alpha and Omega	Revelation 1:8
Mediator between God and Man	II Timothy 2:5
Son of Man	Matthew 18:11
And You Shall Call His Name Jesus	Matthew 1:21
Resurrection and Life	John 11:25
Son of the Highest	Luke 1:32
Prince of Life	Acts 3:15
Lord God Almighty	Revelation 15:3
Root and Offspring of David	Revelation 22:16
Dayspring	Luke 1:78
Lord of All	Acts 10:36
Son of God	John 1:34
Shepherd and Bishop of Your Souls	I Peter 2:25
Chief Cornerstone	Ephesians 2:20
Righteous Judge	II Timothy 4:8
Light of the World	John 8:12
Bright and Morning Star	Revelation 22:16
Head of the Church	Ephesians 1:22
Wonderful, Counselor, Mighty God	Isaiah 9:6
Advocate	I John 2:1

NAMES	MEANING	SCRIPTURE
Jehovah Tsidkenu	The Lord Our Righteousness	Jeremiah 23:6
Jehovah Shammah	The Lord is Present (There)	Ezekiel 48:35
Jehovah Sabaoth	The Lord of Host	I Samuel 1:3
Jehovah M'kaddesh	The Lord Who Sanctifies You	Exodus 31:13
Jehovah Jireh	The Lord Who Sees and Provides	Genesis 22:14
Jehovah Elyon	The Lord Most High	Genesis 14:20
Jehovah Rapha	The Lord Who Heals	Exodus 15:26
Jehovah Elohim	The Lord Our Almighty Creator	Genesis 2:4
Jehovah El Shaddai	The Lord God Almighty	Genesis 17:11
Jehovah Nissi	The Lord Our Banner	Exodus 17:15
Jehovah Rohi	The Lord Our Shepherd	Psalm 23
Jehovah Shalom	The Lord Our Peace	Judges 6:24
Jehovah Mephalti	The Lord My Deliver	Psalm 18:2
Jehovah Moshiekh	The Lord Your Savior and Redeemer	Isaiah 49:26
Jehovah El Nose	The Lord God the Forgives	Psalm 99:8
Jehovah Adonai	The Lord Our Master	Genesis 15:2

God's Blessing

CHAPTER 5

John 11:1-7

> ➢ 1 Now a man named Lazarus was sick. He was from Bethany, the village of Mary and her sister Martha.
> ➢ 2 (This Mary, whose brother Lazarus now lay sick, was the same one who poured perfume on the Lord and wiped his feet with her hair.)
> ➢ 3 So the sisters sent word to Jesus, "Lord, the one you love is sick.
> ➢ 4 When he heard this, Jesus said, "This sickness will not end in death. No, it is for God's glory so that God's Son may be glorified through it."
> ➢ 5 Now Jesus loved Martha and her sister and Lazarus.
> ➢ 6 So when he heard that Lazarus was sick, he stayed where he was two more days,
> ➢ 7 and then he said to his disciples, "Let us go back to Judea."

Blessing! What a misused and misinterpreted word in the body of Christ. I would argue people use this word more than we say Amen or even Jesus at times. How is your mom doing (she is blessed)? How is Pooky doing (he's blessed). The car is blessed, the dog is blessed, and the turtle crossing the street is blessed. Everybody is blessed. Before we examine the above scripture let us tackle the word *blessing*. The dictionary defines blessing as God's favor and protection or grace after a meal. How does the Bible define the word *blessing*? God tells father Abraham in **Genesis 12:2**, "I will make you into a great nation. I will bless you and make you famous, and you will be a blessing to others."

If we look at **Deuteronomy 8:18**, it says, "But thou shalt remember the LORD thy God: for it is he that giveth thee power to get wealth, that he may establish his covenant which he swore unto thy fathers, as it is this day." The blessing is God's favor on your life to prosper. When people see you, they will see how God has elevated you to the top, made you famous and everything you put your hands to shall prosper.

The word even says in **Deuteronomy 28:8**, "The LORD will command the blessing upon you in your barns and in all that you put your hand to, and He will bless you in the land which the LORD your God gives you." The problem with most Christians is that we are not putting our hands to anything. **Deuteronomy 8:18** states that God gives us the power to get wealth. The power is witty inventions, ideas, supernatural ability to do what you could not do. When God's "super" gets on your "natural" you will have the supernatural ability to do things you could not do before God put his ability on your ability. In other words, the blessing takes the work and toil out of something and makes the path smooth. So, when people see you they will see how things in your life are always coming together. Whether it is your business growing, promotion on the job, a wonderful marriage, children doing well, etc. The blessing is when you have nothing missing and nothing broken in your life.

That is why the Word tells us in **Psalm 35:27**, "Let them shout for joy and rejoice, who favor my vindication; and let them say continually, "The LORD be magnified, who delights in the prosperity of His servant."

The blessing will take you from lack to abundance overnight. Let us ponder on what is stated in **Deuteronomy 8:18**. The text says that God gives us the power to get wealth. The irony is that the government has a housing voucher program, commonly referred to as Section 8, which assists low-income families by providing vouchers to rent homes and apartments. But, when we turn to section 8 of Deuteronomy, verse 18, we see that God gives us the power to get wealth and that wealth can be used to buy your own home and own apartment buildings, in cash. The Bible gives us a constant reminder that there are always two systems in operation. The world believes in luck and happenstance, but as believers, we operate under an open heaven. When the blessing is on our lives something that would have failed for someone else will work. An assignment you are given at work that others may have failed at, you will succeed because of God's blessing on your life.

The opening text of this chapter concerning Lazarus is not a commonly used text to reference the blessing. That is what I love about the Lord because He can show us revelation in any passage of scripture. We often wrestle with the issue of a compassionate Jesus who elected to stay two more days knowing his friend Lazarus has died. But, Jesus understands what we often miss; when you have the blessing, everything must come to life around us. The blessing makes all things new and even if something is dead, the blessing can resurrect it. That is why Jesus didn't panic about Lazarus and tells Martha that you will see him again. Martha, like most church folk when things are not going their way, said, sarcastically "I know that he will rise again in the resurrection at the last day." Then Jesus said, "I am the resurrection and the life. He who believes in Me, though he may die, he shall live. And whoever lives and believes in Me shall never die. Do you believe this?"

The power of this story is when He called Lazarus out of the grave He called him by his name if not, everyone that was dead in the area would have risen out of the grave. We would have a New Testament version of Michael Jackson's Thriller video. When you want something, you must be specific so that the blessing can work, specifically. When you have the blessing, you can put the power of God on anything and it will come to life. The blessing is the spiritual defibrillator; it can shock anything dead in your life back to life.

In John 5, Jesus stopped by the pool of Bethesda. In this story, a brother was lying on his bed, sick for 38 years, waiting for someone to put him in the water. How this resembles our own lives when we are stuck in the system. We wait 40 years on a job, waiting for a man to give us a retirement package or our pension. I am not speaking against employment, but how many people are stuck in a rut or a rough place and have been there, generation after generation, waiting for the government to do something, hoping the Democrats or the Republicans will fix it, or maybe they will increase my social security check. How long will we continue to depend on the world's system to get results in our life? How long will we be satisfied with living in Lodebar? In **2 Samuel 9:1**, David asked the question, "Is there yet any that is left of the house of Saul, that I may shew him kindness for Jonathan's sake? They answered and said that Jonathan has a son that is lame and is down in Lodebar (ghetto in biblical times) and his name is Mephibosheth."

Notice what happened after they took Mephibosheth out of the ghetto in verses **6-9**

- 6 Now when Mephibosheth, the son of Jonathan, the son of Saul, was come unto David, he fell on his face and did reverence. And David said, Mephibosheth. And he answered, Behold thy servant!
- 7 And David said unto him, Fear not: for I will surely shew thee kindness for Jonathan thy father's sake and will restore thee all the land of Saul thy father; and thou shalt eat bread at my table continually.
- 8 And he bowed himself, and said, what is thy servant, that thou shouldest look upon such a dead dog as I am?
- 9 Then the king called to Ziba, Saul's servant, and said unto him, I have given unto thy master's son all that pertained to Saul and to all his house."

In one day, Mephibosheth went from the ghetto to the king's palace. That is what happens when the blessing is on your life. Nothing can stop your prosperity, nothing can stop your seed, and nothing can stop your progress. The blessing will chase you down, find you and bring you to a large place. **Psalm 139:8** says, "If I ascend up into heaven, thou art there: if I make my bed in hell, behold, thou art there."

Look at what happens when a sidewalk is made. They pour the concrete, but over time, weeds find a way to come up through the cracks. That is what the blessing does in your life. It does not matter if the enemy tries to put spiritual concrete over your destiny, God's promises will always prevail. On top of that, God is ready to make you laugh, just like Sarah. He is going to do things that you say, I'm too old, or I forgot about that, but God is going to do it because the blessing is on your life.

When Sarah heard that she was about to have a child, the Bible says, in **Genesis 18:12**, that Sarah laughed because of her old age. The blessing is not reliant on your age, the blessing is an arrow shot out of the mouth of God that will not stop until it lands on its target. Think about that for a minute. The blessing will always complete its assignment. Look at what God told Abraham in **Genesis 12:1-3**

- ➢ 1 Now the LORD had said unto Abram, get thee out of thy country, and from thy kindred, and from thy father's house, unto a land that I will shew thee:
- ➢ 2 And I will make of thee a great nation, and I will bless thee, and make thy name great; and thou shalt be a blessing:
- ➢ 3 And I will bless them that bless thee and curse him that curseth thee: and in thee shall all families of the earth be blessed.

You do not have to toil and fight. Just receive. This chapter is vital to my own personal life. I have countless stories of how God has given me favor and supernatural blessings in my life. I have seen God cancel debts. I have walked to a hotel, knowing I did not have a room or a reservation. I didn't have any cash and said in faith, that there is a room in my name and they had a paid-in-full room in my name when I arrived at the front desk. I still, to this day, do not know how that room was available and paid for, but God knows! I spoke out loud that I wanted to speak at a conference in Alaska because I always wanted to go there. While at another conference in West Virginia, I sat at the table with a school administrator from Alaska (you know the rest of the story). I have received favor in the outreaches I do in my community with people freely giving me supplies to support the ministry. I have had countless people put cash in my hand just to be a blessing to me and my family. I share that because I want you to walk in the same divine favor and blessing in your own life. Here are 4 simple steps on how to receive the fullness of God's blessing in your life that I call…

GET R.E.A.L

1. **Receive**: You must learn to receive from God and from man. God wants to bless us and use man (or woman) to get stuff to us, but you cannot be so overly humble and lowly that you curse your own self. You know you need gas and somebody offers you $20, then that is God blessing you but if you say no, then, that is you being stupid. You must learn how to

receive. The root of this is learning that you are worthy, through Christ, and you deserve what He has for you.

2. **Expect**: I expect favor over my life. As I walk into a meeting or a business deal, I'll say to God, give me this opportunity or give me this property that my foot tread upon. I expect favor to show up. Especially, if you are low on cash, you need to be high on faith and favor. Why? Because that is all you have. You must expect everything from a parking spot to a home paid for in cash and beyond.

3. **Anointing**: Understanding that God has a special grace, through His son Jesus, that we are designed to prosper. Through his seed, we are now the seed of Abraham and we have the same blessing that was on Abraham, on our lives. You must understand that everything you do should prosper. If it is not working, ask God if this is His will or show you a different strategy. God has always been faithful by showing me a way out.

4. **Love**: You must love and be thankful for every blessing that God sends your way. Be thankful because thanksgiving will always increase your capacity for more. Learn how to thank God for the parking space, the extra check in the mail, the gas that did not run out before you got home. Love and appreciate everything that God has done and is doing for you and watch how the blessings will overtake you.

God's Deliverance

CHAPTER 6

Psalm 91:15

"He shall call upon me, and I will answer him: I will be with him in trouble; I will deliver him, and honour him."

When I think of the blessing, especially in battles and enlarging their territory, you cannot overlook Joshua. The first chapter of **Joshua, verses 1:8**, start off by saying,

"This book of the law shall not depart from your mouth, but you shall meditate on it day and night, so that you may be careful to do according to all that is written in it; for then you will make your way prosperous, and then you will have success."

Joshua started off with the recipe of success and the special enablement from God to overcome. His blessing was so strong on Joshua and God's people, examine what Rahab the Harlot said about them in **Joshua 2:9-12**

- ➤ 8 Before the men lay down, she came up to them on the roof
- ➤ 9 and said to the men, I know that the LORD has given
- ➤ you the land, and that the fear of you has fallen upon us, and that all the inhabitants of the land melt away before you.
- ➤ 10 For we have heard how the LORD dried up the water of the Red Sea before you when you came out of Egypt, and what you did to the two kings of the Amorites who were

> beyond the Jordan, to Sihon and Og, whom you devoted to destruction.
> 11 And as soon as we heard it, our hearts melted, and there was no spirit left in any man because of you, for the LORD your God, he is God in the heavens above and on the earth beneath.
> 12 Now then, please swear to me by the LORD that, as I have dealt kindly with you, you also will deal kindly with my father's house, and give me a sure sign."

Did you catch what she said in verse 11, how when they heard the word their hearts melted? When was the last time God did something in your life to make your heart melt? When was the last time you read your bible and your heart melted? When God had delivered you out of sickness, debt, divorce, lack, depression, taking all types of medicines, etc., your heart will melt. Your heart has not melted because you have seen God do it in other people's lives, but you have not truly experienced a breakthrough in your own life, yet. It's time for you to experience God's deliverance yourself. God wants to bring you out and deliver you today.

Psalm 66:10-12 says,

> 10 For thou, O God, hast proved us: thou hast tried us, as silver is tried.
> 11 Thou broughtest us into the net; thou laidst affliction upon our loins.

> 12 Thou hast caused men to ride over our heads; we went through fire and through water: but thou broughtest us out into a wealthy place."

I speak over your life that it is your time to be delivered and God does not need months, or years to do it. God can change your situation in one day or even one second. When all the kings came together to fight Joshua and the children of Israel, the Lord said in **Joshua 11:6**, "Then the LORD said to Joshua, "Do not be afraid because of them, for tomorrow at this time I will deliver all of them slain before Israel; you shall hamstring their horses and burn their chariots with fire." In one day, God destroyed their enemies. Here are three highlights of what God has done in one day:

1. Moses parts the Red Sea and the children of Israel are delivered. "Then Moses stretched out his hand over the sea, and all that night the Lord drove the sea back with a strong east wind and turned it into dry land. The waters were divided, and the Israelites went through the sea on dry ground, with a wall of water on their right and on their left." **Exodus 16:21**

2. Delivered Daniel out of the Lion's Den: "Daniel answered, "May the king live forever! My God sent his angel, and he shut the mouths of lions. They have not hurt me, because I was found innocent in His sight. Nor have I ever done any wrong before you, Your Majesty." **Daniel 6:21-22**

3. Delivered Shadrach, Meshach, and Abednego: Nebuchadnezzar declared, "Blessed be the God of Shadrach,

Meshach, and Abednego, who has sent His Angel and delivered His servants who trusted in Him. They violated the king's command and risked their lives rather than serve or worship any god except their own God. **Daniel 3:28**

Even with Shadrach, Meshach, and Abednego, the text in **Daniel 3:19**, shows how Nebuchadnezzar was so furious that they wouldn't bow, that he insisted the fire was turned up 7 times hotter than normal. Here is a simple question, how hot does fire have to be to burn you? That is what the enemy tries to do in our lives, he tries to turn up the pressure, so you will bow to the world's system. You give your tithes and your roof starts leaking. You sow a seed and you get an unexpected bill the very next day. You get off your knees from praying and soaking in the presence of God and the bill collector's start calling and harassing you. Why does this happen? The enemy is trying to get you to bow. Mark my words, we are living in the end times and you will see increasingly more pressure to bow and blend in with the world. It is hard nowadays to distinguish the believer from the nonbeliever. Everyone is drinking together, smoking together, listening to the same secular music together so it is hard to distinguish between the two. I heard someone say that if you wrestle with a pig, chances are you will smell like the pig before the pig smells like you. The enemy wants to put so much pressure on you to bow, but the good news is if you do not bow, then you will not burn. I said if you do not bow, then you will not burn. It's only when you give in to the world's way of doing things that you get burned because things never turn out like you expected. Promotion is on the other side of the furnace! I will say that again, promotion is on the other side of the furnace! You may ask why God allowed you to go through the fire. My response is that it does not matter; what matters is that He delivered you. The verse at the beginning of this chapter in Psalm 91 states that God will deliver and honor us. Look, if you are drowning does it matter who saves you, whether it is the lifeguard or a random person? We become so focused on the why, but we do not understand that God is a delivering God. You cannot be delivered, if you are not in something. As a believer, especially, you will always have opportunities for God to show Himself strong in your life. Stop getting mad this or that happened, embrace the obstacle, look to the hills from whence cometh your help, and onward Christian soldier.

Allow me to share with you my favorite scripture on God's deliverance.

Psalm 91

- He that dwelleth in the secret place of the Most High shall abide under the shadow of the Almighty.
- I will say of the LORD, He is my refuge and my fortress: my God; in him will I trust.
- Surely, he shall deliver thee from the snare of the fowler, and from the noisome pestilence.
- He shall cover thee with his feathers, and under his wings shalt thou trust: his truth shall be thy shield and buckler.
- Thou shalt not be afraid for the terror by night; nor for the arrow that flieth by day;

- Nor for the pestilence that walketh in darkness; nor for the destruction that wasteth at noonday.
- A thousand shall fall at thy side, and ten thousand at thy right hand; but it shall not come nigh thee.
- Only with thine eyes shalt thou behold and see the reward of the wicked.
- Because thou hast made the LORD, which is my refuge, even the Most High, thy habitation;
- There shall no evil befall thee, neither shall any plague come nigh thy dwelling.
- For he shall give his angels charge over thee, to keep thee in all thy ways.
- They shall bear thee up in their hands, lest thou dash thy foot against a stone.
- Thou shalt tread upon the lion and adder: the young lion and the dragon shalt thou trample under feet.
- Because he hath set his love upon me, therefore will I deliver him: I will set him on high, because he hath known my name.
- He shall call upon me, and I will answer him: I will be with him in trouble; I will deliver him, and honour him.
- With long life will I satisfy him and shew him my salvation.

I shared this passage because I pray this prayer just about every single day over my life. About 13 years ago, while riding my motorcycle, the Holy Spirit urged me to start reciting this prayer while riding. Less than 5 minutes later, cars began to slow down and I overreacted. I grabbed my front brake and flipped off my bike. I feared for my life, right in the middle of rush hour traffic. I thought I was going to get run over. After I tumbled, I quickly got up and ran off the highway. There, I collapsed in the grass. People ran to my attention and then I was rushed to the hospital. I thought I was dying. At the end of the night, I walked away with no broken bones and only three stitches. Yes, my body ached, but no bones were broken.

Psalm 34:20 says, "He keeps all his bones; not one of them is broken." Won't He do it! You must understand that whatever situation you are facing right now, God is your source. I want to speak to the brother or sister, who lives from paycheck to paycheck, or maybe you're unemployed or just in bondage to not enough. I understand when the weight of bills, obligations, family, and kids can result in tremendous stress. Moving from this place of stress to God's place of peace is one of the greatest challenges you will face in this journey, but it is the one thing your life and destiny depends on. Even the children of Israel didn't want to get off the system.

Exodus 16:2-3

> ➢ And the whole congregation of the children of Israel murmured against Moses and Aaron in the wilderness:
> ➢ And the children of Israel said unto them, would that we had died by the hand of the LORD in the land of Egypt, when we sat by the flesh-pots, and when we did eat bread to the full; for ye have brought us forth into this wilderness, to kill this whole assembly with hunger.

When you try to take people off the system they will fight you or say the preacher is just trying to get your money or church people are trifling. When you try to get people a better job, they say it will affect their rent amount in their government housing. You try to take them off food stamps, they feel like they will not be able to eat. Someone people do not even know how to buy groceries without an EBT card. Some people would rather die on a job and live in fear instead of stepping out in faith and launching a business that God has called them to. Let me serve as your modern-day Moses for a moment and let you know that I am here to set you free from your mental Egypt. You cannot come from out of bondage until you decide to leave Egypt. God has your promise land waiting, but you must be willing to let go of Pharaoh.

Pastor Bill Winston talked about how the enemy wants to own three things in your life: the mill, the money, and the marketplace. The mill is the place you work, money is how you are paid and what you use to exchange and purchase goods in the marketplace. If the enemy controls the mill, then he can make you work overtime or work on Sundays. Then as soon as you get more money, inflation will go up, interest rates will increase, along with bread and milk. So, any raise you get will be diminished when you go into the marketplace. If you are stuck on this system, you will forever go around and around on this hamster wheel and never get off.

Allow me to show you how to get off the system and break free from Egypt. God has given me a 7-step process that will take you from where you are to where you need to be. This is a God-breathed process, that the Lord showed me through seeking Him on how to get people off this system. I wanted God to give me a plan for the individual who has tried other methods and programs and still is not where they need to be. Finally, it is time for you to do it God's way. With God's way, you do not need any other way.

Saturate yourself with these seven steps and watch God move in your finances like never before. This is how we operate in our own lives and I would never want to share something with you that I could not first do myself. This is the "Get Off The System Plan" and it is called…**F.R.E.E.D.O.M.**

LETTER	MEANING	GET OFF THE SYSTEM PRINCIPLE	SCRIPTURE REF
F	FIRST FRUIT	GOD'S BLESSING	Malachi 3:8-11
R	REAL ESTATE	GOD'S ENTREPRENEUR	Psalm 24:1
E	EVERYTHING HAS A BUDGET	GOD'S ECONOMY	Psalm 103:19
E	EMERGENCY FUND	GOD'S ABUNDANCE	Proverbs 13:11
D	DESTROY DEBT	GOD'S DELIVERANCE	Romans 13:8
O	OPERATE BELOW SEA LEVEL	GOD'S PROMISE	1 Timothy 5:8
M	MASTER MONEY	GOD'S LABOR	Proverbs 27:23

F: First Fruits

"Will a man rob God? Yet you have robbed Me! But you say, 'In what way have we robbed You?' In tithes and offerings.

- ➢ You are cursed with a curse, for you have robbed Me, even this whole nation.
- ➢ Bring all the tithes into the storehouse, that there may be food in My house, and try Me now in this," Says the

> LORD of hosts, "If I will not open for you the windows of heaven and pour out for you such a blessing that there will not be room enough to receive it.
> And I will rebuke the devourer for your sakes, so that he will not destroy the fruit of your ground, nor shall the vine fail to bear fruit for you in the field," says the LORD of hosts.

Malachi 3:8-11

This is the first pillar of your financial success. Tithing or giving your first fruits to God. As you begin your financial journey, understand that tithing is the first pillar for a specific reason. Tithing, as we previously discussed, is the key ingredient to get you on the path of financial prosperity. Tithing is not the end all; rather, it is the key that unlocks the door to God's abundance. Tithing is the first step. Tithing is giving 10% of your gross income and/or paycheck to God.

Example: if your paycheck (gross before anything is taken out) is $1000. Then your tithe would be $100. Let us take that same $1000 check, after taxes, the amount you bring home, for instance, is $750…your tithe is still $100. Why, because we want to give God a tithe out of what our total income is, not just what's left over.

Some people use the logic that they will tithe off their net (what they bring home) and then again when they get their income tax refund just in case they missed something. One of the main problems in the body of Christ is that we are always looking for shortcuts to God's blessings. You must do everything with integrity and recognize that you need to tithe off your gross and every increase that comes your way. If someone gives you $20, tithe $2. You get a refund, you tithe off it. You get that big insurance claim of 1 million dollars, then you tithe $100,000. When you are faithful with little, God will give you much. If you are faithfully tithing off that $1000 check, then your spirit and mind will not have any problems tithing off the $100,000 check or the 1-million-dollar check.

The tithe we subscribed to as the seed of Abraham is not under the law but is a law. A law is an established principle that will work for anyone who puts it to use. Gravity is a law. That is why an unbeliever can tithe or give large sums of money to charities and continue to prosper. If you have ever been in the place as described in **Haggai 1:6**, "You have sown much, and harvested little. You eat, but you never have enough; you drink, but you never have your fill. You clothe yourselves, but no one is warm. And he who earns wages does so to put them into a bag with holes" then you need to tithe.

Tithing is not something that is just done out of vain repetition, but every tithe, I do not care how long you tithe, is our covenant connection to God and is not to be taken lightly. When you tithe, you are reminded that God will come in and rebuke every devourer in your finances and in your life. I know what it's like to have $40 and as soon as I get it, something will come up that cost $38 dollars or to have $100 and you must do something on the car that cost $98.15. When the devourer is in your life, what you have is already immediately eaten up. If you feel as though you continue to get bill after bill or there is 'always something' then that is a prime case in point of the devourer in operation. Or when you have saved $500 and something 'unexpected' comes up and takes your entire savings. That, my friend, is the devourer. It is a subtle spirit sent by Satan because you have a crack in your foundation.

Tithing revokes the enemy's access into your finances. The first wall of resistance against this teaching is that "I cannot afford to tithe!" My response is you cannot afford to tithe because you have not been tithing! If you had been tithing your financial situation would be different. Some people teach the concept of just tithe what you can until you get to 10%. When you go to Walmart, and your groceries are $200, does the cashier say, "Oh, just pay what you can sweetheart and if you do not have $200 you can still take all the food home." Let me help you with the answer, NO, that will not happen, especially at Walmart. If you do not have it, you will be putting some food back until it matches what you do have.

When you tithe, you tell Satan and the mammon system that you are vacating the premises and moving to God's system. But you are not just giving money to a church, you are sowing your faith into God's system. Yes, your tithe should go to your local church, not your favorite TV preacher or even charity. I am teaching this book from the perspective that you are a believer and as believers we should have a local fellowship.

Step one takeaway:

Tithe 10% of your gross to your local fellowship. If you are self-employed with a more sporadic income schedule, then tithe when the income comes in. If you are on fixed income or receive disability, tithe off whatever you get or comes in. From babysitting money to an inheritance from grandma, tithe. When you give, don't eyeball the collection plate as it makes its way throughout the church. Instead, release it! Many people tithe but still struggle financially because all they have done was give money with their hands. They have never released the seed in their heart. If I held onto a collard green seed that I had not yet planted into the ground, then I'd never yield any collards. You must release your faith with your tithes and know in your heart that God is going to give you a blessing (ability to prosper) and close the access to the devourer because I tithe. I can sense that as soon as you read this, you cringe at the idea of giving, not because you do not want to, but you are afraid of how you are going to make it when everything is already tight. This is what the bible describes as the "good fight of faith." For me to say that from the moment you start tithing, money will be deposited into your bank account out of nowhere would be misleading and dishonest. No, the enemy will try to come against you. Especially your mind because you are leaving him and his system as your source and switching to God's system.

Here is what I do know; I have never read about or met anyone who tithed while trusting God with their finances who has ever regretted it. Give God six months and I commit to you that you will have less stress with the 90% than you did with the 100%. Try God in this and watch the devourer be removed from your life.

R: Real Estate

"The earth is the LORD'S, and the fullness thereof; the world, and they that dwell therein." **Psalm 24:1**

If the earth is the Lord's and the Lord is our father, then it would only make sense for us to share in this ownership. It has been said that more millionaires have been made from real estate investing than any other business or opportunity. Real estate investing has been a long-time strategy of mine as a wealth builder. My partner and I, along with our spouses started a real estate company well over 15 years ago. We have been landlords, sold properties and now we are moving into flipping properties.

As a part of your get-of-out-lack plan, I strongly suggest real estate be a part of your plan. This subject is much more detailed and involved than I could cover in this book, but I will do my best to simplify the subject. Let me share 5 simple steps to get you started on buying your first rental property:

1. Buy a single-family home

    A. Less maintenance
    B. Manage it like you would manage your home
    C. Fewer tenants
    D. After initial repairs, minimum upkeep
    E. Various finance options

2. Finance the Loan

    A. Conventional Financing (10% percent down (may vary) + closing costs)

B. Can be treated like a second home
C. With high credit scores you can get sometimes get up to 104%-106% financing
D. Owner financing-this is where someone owns the home and you set up an agreement with them to pay them monthly payments to buy it. This is sometimes referred to as rent-to-own or a lease-option. This is a great way to purchase properties (we used this to purchase our duplexes) without having to go to a bank and get approved
E. Turn your first home into an investment property (rent it out/purchase another)
F. Equity Lines of Credit
G. Credit Cards
H. Investment Accounts (401K, Self-Directed IRA)-you can use money from these accounts to cover down payment, purchase properties outright or finance the rehab

3. Make an Offer

    A. Contact the real estate agent listed or the home owner
    B. Inquire about the asking price
    C. Ask about buyer incentives (closing cost, home warranty, etc.)
    D. View the property with the agent
    E. Take someone with you, if necessary, who can estimate repair cost, like a licensed contractor, not just your buddy from church

Base your offer on the following **example:**

- Asking Price: $50,000
- Estimated Repairs: $5,000
F. Offer Price: $45,000 (maximum amount you should offer)- always factor in other items like taxes, property management fees, lawn care, etc. You can never be too conservative when considering your cost
G. Always get a home inspection-this will tell you if something is wrong with the house. Everything you cannot see up front, so a home inspector will check out the house from top to bottom
H. Agree to close 45-60 days from the date of the contract

4. Find Good Tenants

   A. Section 8 Tenants-tenants who get a voucher for their monthly rent. There should be a housing authority office that has a list of tenants. Your home will have to be inspected first and then put on their available properties list
   B. Tenants on disability-they get a monthly check and it is sometimes paid by an outside agency which means you will always get paid
   C. Elderly Tenants-they are normally very good about always paying their rent on time
   D. Married Couples-they do not always have other living options, so they will often make the sacrifices necessary to pay that rent
   E. No children-I am not against children, but be mindful that children are children

F. No pets-I stay away from all pets, period
G. Steady employment and gross income are 3 times the monthly rent-depending on the clientele (we did low to mid income), you may have to overlook some credit issues and even income ratio issues
H. Place "For Rent" sign in the window or front yard with a tube that will have your leases for people to take one out
I. Use an organization like the National Tenant Network to screen tenants-they will charge a minimal fee and you can get the credit and criminal background of the tenant you are screening
J. Charge application fee-typically $30-$35 for one person and $55 for two people

5. Eviction Process-this is an overview, but you will have to take the time to learn about the eviction process in your state. This was based on our experience in the state of Virginia.

A. Rent is due between the 1st and the 5th
B. 10% late fee on anything posted and received after the 5th (rent received with reservation is a legal term that should be used on your receipts. This allows you to always pursue judgment and possession if the moment arises.)
C. Send rent reminder on the 8th
D. Send five day pay or quit notice on the 10th -this document is a letter that tells the tenant they have 5 days to bring their balance current or the eviction process will start

E. Fill out an unlawful detainer on the 16th this is completed at the court house and has a fee that is determined by your local jurisdiction. The form is a legal document stating
F. that the tenants are living there illegally since they have not paid their rent. After you fill out this form they will give you a court date, typically a few weeks out
G. Court-this is where you finally have your date in court with the judge to ask for judgment (of the debt owed) and possession of the property
H. Writ of Possession-This is an additional document that is often filled out at the sheriff's office when you have received possession of the property from the judge, but the tenant has refused to move out voluntarily. The sheriff will come, and help "facilitate" the move.

Pros and cons of real estate investing:

Pros...

- Positive cash flow
- Appreciating asset
- Leverage from properties to purchase other properties
- Leverage assets to pay down costly consumer debt
- Build long-term wealth
- Great rate of return (out paces stock market, inflation and most other investments)

Cons...

- Upfront cost

- Maintenance Cost (plumbing problems, etc.)
- Unexpected cost (broken windows, roof repair, etc.)
- Vacancies
- Court Cost/Appearances
- Time Commitment (court, viewing properties, etc.)

Real estate is one of the key ingredients that I use to build my own personal wealth and to pass on a legacy to my family. One of the key obstacles people face is how to get started and the having the money to get started. One of the suggestions that I have is turn your current home (if you own one) into a rental property and purchase another home. If you do not own a home or you are not able to do this, look at other options. You may have some money in your 401(k) or from insurance that you can use to put a down payment on a rental property or to cover the repair cost.

For the person who says I do not own a home, or I just do not have the money, there are a couple of ways to get started. One, I suggest joining a local real estate group in your area where you can network and find private investors (hard money lenders) who may be willing to lend you money based on a deal you find. You can also gain money by helping people to find deals (bird dogging) or connecting investors with buyers. There are always ways to get started.

Do not use not having any money as an excuse to get started. There are so many ways from owner financing, to private lenders that if you want it bad enough it will happen. There is a poem I learned many years ago that says:

"Excuses are tools of incompetence that build monuments of nothingness and those that so often use them, rarely accomplish anything." Make deals and not excuses. What I am sharing with you requires sweat equity. Tithing is going to require effort and real estate is going to require effort. But without struggle, there is no progress. You must realize that you are going to have to put in some work to change your situation. Change is not change until it is changed. Now, it's time for you to change.

E: Everything has a place in your budget

"The LORD hath prepared his throne in the heavens; and his kingdom ruleth over all." **Psalm 103:19**

There are many systems and kingdoms of this world. If you remember before Jesus started his ministry in Matthew 4, he was fasting 40 days in the wilderness. In **Matthew 4:8-9**, Satan says:

> ➢ 8 Again, the devil taketh him up into an exceeding high mountain, and sheweth him all the kingdoms of the world, and the glory of them;
> ➢ 9 And saith unto him, All these things will I give thee, if thou wilt fall down and worship me."

The enemy makes this offer to countless people, especially Christians, all the time. If you stop singing for the church and take this R&B contract, I will bless you and you can give more money to your church. If you stop dancing for the church and dance for this secular group, I will bless you. I am not speaking about Christians being in the marketplace, I am speaking on how the enemy uses the systems of the world to lure Christians with the temptation of fame, wealth and endless opportunity. We have placed the systems or kingdoms of the world, higher than God's kingdom. In layman's terms, doing it God's way is less profitable (in the world's eyes) than doing it the world's way.

In **Psalm 103:19**, we see that God's kingdom (or His system) rules overall and is far better than the world's kingdom. If you only measure the success of a kingdom by the amount of money or fame, then you are missing it. Let us examine the countless people who took the deal of Satan's kingdom and look how their life has changed or ended. Drugs, suicide, bad deals, bankruptcy, multiple divorces and ruined careers. I cannot tell you the number of times you see a famous person on TV only to find out they have very little money in the bank, struggling to pay child support, or essentially living from check to check.

"For what shall it profit a man, if he shall gain the whole world, and lose his own soul?" **Mark 8:36**. In God's system, He is building your spiritual man and your natural man. **3 John 2:2** says, Beloved, I wish above all things that thou mayest prosper and be in health, even as thy soul prospereth."

In God's system, you are being developed to finish well in life on this side of heaven and to live eternally with God on the other side of heaven. My football coach would say, "It is not how you start, but how you finish." The world's kingdoms are nothing more than a counterfeit structure set up by Satan. Satan tries to distort God's system and His world because only God has creative ability. God is the creator and Satan is nothing more than a washed up and angry minister of music who was a former employee of God. Now his entire modus operandi is to lure as many people as possible to His system to prevent them from truly experiencing God in their lives.

The law of environment says that your environment will change you before you change it. This happens to so many Christians who leave God's system and go to the world's system. The world changes them, and they become a carnal Christian at best, but many stray from the faith. You may ask, then what does this have to do with the statement of everything has a place in your budget.

The short answer is, everything. When you understand that you are building a budget with God as the center and now you do not have a selfish approach to money but a Godly approach. When you have a kingdom minded budget, you will look to sow more and give more to other ministries and missions before you upgrade to leather seats on another car you cannot afford. A kingdom minded budget understands that God is the owner of all. One thing I have noticed in the body of Christ is that many people think they are off the hook once they give their 10% and they can do what they want with the 90% percent. They could not be further from the truth.

Just to be clear, God owns everything. The 10% is what you owe Him and what he requires off the top. The 90% is what He has entrusted you with and expects you to be a good steward over.

Many Christians tithe but still struggle financially because they have lost the battle of the 90%. They have mixed bad teaching and faith and never yielded any results. Someone told you to name it and claim it, but they didn't tell you that you still must pay that light bill or make the car payment. As a result, you made confessions as the repo man picked up your car. You said it was the enemy attacking you. The real enemy is inner me. The real enemy is your inability to manage what God has entrusted you with. As famed teacher Myles Munroe stated, "The only reason Christians need miracles is because they cannot manage what God has given them." The 90% must have a high level of accountability and stewardship. Walking by faith does not give you a pass to not manage your pocketbook.

In terms of budgeting, I can talk in lengths about this subject. I would encourage you, especially if you belong to a church to consider bringing me in to discuss these pillars in more depth. You can contact my ministry, The Empowerment Zone at our website: *www.empowerlives.net* for more information and to fill out our contact form.

In budgeting, there are many systems and "experts" that you can find. You can find countless articles and books on the internet. Let us keep it simple. Use an excel spreadsheet (what I use) or get a sheet of paper. Write down every expense you have for the month. A good way to do this is to go a month or so and keep a receipt, if possible, of every dollar you spend. You want to write down everything from hair/nails to when you eat out at lunch. Account for gas, money spent at the snack machine and everything you paid that month. When you total this up, you will get an idea of what you spend each month. Look at the sample budget (spending plan) included. Some people like to call it a spending plan of how to use the 90% because a budget seems too restrictive.

This is just an instance of how you can organize your finances. There are countless apps as well as software to make it effortless. For me, I have used excel for years. I can see everything right in front of me and make necessary tweaks. When you have your total expenses laid out in front of you, you then know where you stand; or, if you are spending 110% of what you make.

Example: You may bring home $5000 per month after taxes, but you're spending $5500 per month. That is why you bounce checks, or your account may stay in the negative. You may be using credit cards instead of cash. The Bible says without a vision the people perish, and in the natural, without a budget the people perish. You must keep track of what you spend. No exceptions! Stop saying you are on a fixed income. When you start operating within these principles, God can unfix your income.

Assign a category for the money you spend. Map out the estimated amounts for each category for the month. If you have everything listed in a category, when you get paid, you will not just run to the mall, you will run to your budget to ensure that you have budgeted for the mall. This is not about me being cheap; rather, it's about me teaching you that you can do whatever you want if your budget allows, and you have your priorities straight. But do not have your nails "did" and your lights are off and your gas tank on E. Instead, maybe just get your hands done and not your feet this time so you can pay the light bill and fill up your tank. If things are tight, get out the polish at home and take care of everything else.

SAMPLE MONTHLY BUDGET

Paycheck	Estimate
Job #1: Total Gross Income (before taxes)	$5,000.00
Take home pay after deductions	-$1,200.00
Income Total	$3,800.00

JULY BUDGET	Estimate	**BALANCE** Amount	**NOTES** Due Date
Tithes (off of your gross)	$500.00		
Rent/Mortgage	$850.00	$150,000.00	1st
Savings	$200.00		
Life Insurance	$55.00		1st
Groceries	$350.00		
Gas	$90.00		
Car Payment	$325.00	$17,000.00	15th
Car Insurance	$150.00		15th
Car Maintenance	$80.00		
Renter's/Homeowner's Insurance	$45.00		10th
Cell Phone Bill	$105.00		7th
Cable Bill	$175.00		28th
Gas Bill	$50.00		28th
Water Bill	$60.00		
Electric Bill	$75.00		8th
Credit Card	$115.00	$1,255.00	6th
Hair/Nails	$150.00		
Clothes	$100.00		
Gym Membership	$30.00		25th
Entertainment	$75.00		
Vacation Fund	$100.00		
Christmas Fund	$50.00		
Additional Bill #1	$35.00	$627.00	30th
Additional Bill #2	$35.00	$591.00	30th

Total Expenses	$3,800.00	
Total Income	$3,800.00	$169,473.00
Total Money Left Over	$0	

Why should I have a budget?

- It tracks your spending (you cannot keep track of everything in your head).
- It allows you to see where your money is going.
- It helps you when you need to cut back in certain areas to free up money in other areas.
- It helps you to become organized and responsible as well as be a good steward over your money.

SUGGESTIONS:

- Keep a small memo pad with you and write down the things that you purchase daily. This helps you to watch your spending.
- Keep all receipts and organize them by month. Keep the receipts in separate envelopes or a folder.
- Organize all your bills into different categories (credit cards, utilities, etc.) Also, you can separate them by the time of the month in which you pay the bill. Bills should not be laying all over the house and on the floor. Some people even use a bill calendar to help them.
- Organize your personal information by putting it into folders (ex. Bank statements, pay stubs, etc.).
- Put your important documents into a binder. It is helpful when everything is together in one place.
- Try to save at least 10% of what your make.

- Set up goals for your budget and always look for ways to cut back.
- Pray to God for wisdom before working on your budget.
- The household finances should include both spouses (both individuals need to be on the same page).
- Ask for wisdom in your giving…just because we are Christians, it does not mean that we must give our house, car, money for our children's education, and everything else away, every time someone asks for something.
- Stop worrying about everyone else's financial situation and concentrate on you and your house!
- Get your life in order, because you do not want your finances cursed or interrupted because your walk with Christ is not inline. Sin is the mother of all poverty.
- Recite the phrase below daily:

"It is not the will of God for me to be in debt. In the name of Jesus, I bind the stronghold (debt) in my household. I confess that I am blessed, and I have plenty more to put in store. Wealth and riches are stored up for me. Millions, billions, and trillions is what God has for me!"

You must assign a dollar to everything that comes through your household to become an excellent steward. I have become extremely proficient at this over the years and I have learned that there will always be unexpected items from time to time, but hard work does pay off. When you plan what is coming in, in advance, it takes a lot of stress off what to do when you get your check because you already have a plan. There are three scenarios or categories that you will fall into once you start doing your budget:

Scenario #1: You have more expenses than income

This is the situation that many people find themselves in. Now, you can see why you are overextended and stressed out every month because you don't want to face the music. But now that you see it on paper, it is painful. It is not about how much money you make, it's all about how much money you keep. I speak from experience. This is where you must learn how to become meticulous about your expenses; plus, meticulous about putting God first and trusting Him. Naturally, this spot is frustrating and can feel hopeless at times, but **Luke 1:37** reminds us that "with God nothing is impossible." In this position, the first thing you want to do is repent to God for allowing your finances to get out of control and not being an excellent steward. Next, you want to go through your expenses and see what you can cut or eliminate. Some things will hurt because you have built a lifestyle and image around overspending and now you must change. That could mean downsizing your house or cars, cutting out cable or reducing your package, cutting out gym memberships and even the dry cleaners. It may mean painting your nails and doing your own hair for a while. It may mean saying no to the mall and yes to staying home and eating a home cooked meal. It may mean you cannot go out to eat with everyone after church but go home.

Pastors, this is for you, as well. Spiritual leaders can be the worst at this because they often want to portray a certain image to never give off the impression that they are on a budget or have money concerns. If you fall into this scenario where you are overextended, use yourself as motivation and a testimony to help others in your congregation to get out of debt and break through into abundance. On the contrary, you must learn to create more income. Sometimes, you can just adjust the withholdings you have for taxes. Instead of getting a large refund, increase your withholdings and you will get more; if not, all the money owed you from the year. It may mean getting a part time job at the hardware store or the grocery store. If you are married it could mean, a spouse who wasn't working may now have to go to work or do something part time to chip in. Regardless, you must do what you have to do. The key thing in this process is this, do not add any more expenses. Stay away from the credit cards and do not borrow or file bankruptcy. If you stay firm in this process and do not add more expenses, in a matter of time you will pay down and pay off your debts.

A key ingredient is to list all your bills (debts) and any balances owed and any extra money you have put towards those debts. Some people would say pay off the smallest first, while others say pay off the highest interest first. My approach is to take care of your basic needs; clothing, housing, transportation, utilities, and legal obligations (ex. Attorney bills, IRS, judgements) and then everything else. If you can't meet your basic needs, you will be stressed. If your utilities are cut off, you will be stressed. If you don't take care of your legal obligations, they can garnish your wages or freeze your bank account and you will be stressed. So, handle your business first in these areas. One last thing; do not stop tithing! When you are faithful when money is tight, God will make space for you and what used to be tight will become a great space.

Scenario #2: Your expenses and income are equal

This is not a bad place to be. You may feel like you have just enough but trust me you will be fine. In this place, the first thing you want to do is go through your expenses and see if you can reduce or eliminate any expenses. By reducing at least one expense, you will immediately be in the black or in surplus. Secondly, do not and I repeat, do not add any new expenses. I cannot tell you the number of times people look at their money and try to add another expense because they "think" they can handle it. In this position, you want to continue to minimize the expenses and look for other ways to grow your income. Whether it's additional education (try to do it debt free), getting a part time job or starting a business on the side. Now, is the time to grow your income to create further separation between what is coming in and what is going out. In addition to tithing, you can look to set more money aside for offerings and additional giving, after you have eliminated even more expenses. With a kingdom mindset, you will look to see who you can bless first before buying something for yourself.

Scenario #3: Your expenses are less than your income

Welcome to abundance. This is the place that we need to be and remain in the kingdom of God. We will always have expenses (ex. lights, water, etc.), but we do not always have to have debt (ex. car notes, mortgages, etc.). At this place, look to see how you can be an even greater blessing to others and the kingdom of God. With the extra money you can look to start other businesses, buy real estate, give to missionaries and fund ministry projects. Do not stop here, continuously grow your income so you can become a kingdom millionaire and a kingdom billionaire who is able to finance the kingdom of God. This is the place that God wants all of us.

That is why He said in **John 10:10**, "I came that they may have and enjoy life, and have it in abundance [to the full, till it overflows]." In conclusion, whichever scenario you are, especially scenario 1 and 2, be encouraged and know that God is your source and He is a deliverer. I love how the New Jerusalem Bible states **Psalm 107:13-14**, "They cried out to Yahweh in their distress, he rescued them from their plight, he brought them out from gloom and shadow dark as death and shattered their chains." God is going to shatter your chains of lack and not enough. Today is your day.

E: Emergency Fund

"Wealth gotten by vanity shall be diminished: but he that gathereth by labour shall increase." **Proverbs 13:11**

I remember seeking the Lord one time concerning my own finances and some challenges that I was facing. I asked the Lord what I was missing in my finances. I gave, tithed and budgeted. The Holy Spirit said one thing thou lackest (reminds me of the rich young ruler story), you do not have anything saved. No savings is often the root of your problems. When you do not have anything to draw from financially, you now must rely on God for a miracle or a credit card, payday loan, or a friend to get you through.

This text in **Proverbs 13:11** is important because when we learn to save little by little, it will grow exponentially. My Grandma Manley would always tell me, "son, save something for a rainy day." By a show of hands, who has ever experienced a rainy day? It will rain but when you have savings, it will serve as your umbrella. Often when I talk with people about money, it is not the big spiritual things they are missing; rather, it is basic things like not saving. When you save, you are not putting your trust into money. Instead, you are operating in wisdom and reducing the financial risk of future events.

Example: if your car needs hundreds of dollars' worth of repairs in the future, you can pull from your savings if your budget cannot cover it. Your life does not have to be disrupted. Savings; it's amazing how sometimes the more money we make, the less we save. This is the reason budgets are so critical. You must make savings a priority. You must save something regardless, even if it is only five dollars a month. Put it under your mattress, in an old water jug, hide it, just save it. Saving and having savings is often the difference between financial stress and financial peace. This applies to ministries as well. We have money flowing in and out, but nothing set aside for emergencies. Instead, we must sell chicken dinners to fix the roof and have special services to cover the cost of the needed repairs. Savings allow us to be in a better position to pass on an inheritance to our children. It positions us for business opportunities when they arise. How many times have you seen an opportunity pass through your hands because you "just" didn't have it? You have even said, "Man, if I had it, I would have bought that…" You must save and become diligent in your saving.

I suggest at least 2 types of savings accounts.

1. You need to have an immediate emergency fund. Some people say $1000, others say $3500. I say, one month of your expenses is a good amount to strive for. So, if you know you have $5000 a month in expenses, then, that should be your goal for your immediate savings account. Some people may argue that it may take them forever to save this amount; however, you need a target. Having one month of expenses saved is a good comfort level for you and your peace of mind. Plus, if something comes up and you must use some of it, you are still ok. Just work quickly to build it back up.
2. The next savings account should be 6-8 months of expenses saved. So, if your expenses are $5000 per month, then your goal in this savings account should be 30K-40K saved.

First, before you question how you can do this, understand that you must have a plan. People do not plan to fail, they just fail to plan. The old African proverb says, "Going slow does not keep you from arriving." Remember you are reducing expenses, getting a part time job, starting a business, etc. As you get extra income you can take a portion of that income and put it towards your savings goal. There is nothing more satisfying than knowing you can pay for an unexpected expense and it will not eat through your entire budget. Friends, I call that… financial peace; to know that God is my source and I have money saved to handle the challenges of life. So, if I lose my job, it is disappointing, but I know I can still eat and pay my bills because I have some money set aside. In terms of saving, we can have a healthy discussion about what percentage to save, but what matters most is that you save something. In a perfect situation, you want to save at least 10% of what you bring home. That is not always feasible depending on what scenario you fall into. My counsel to you is to save something and be consistent, at a minimum, with that amount. So, do not save $500 per month but you end up spending $495 of that every month. You are better off saving $5 per month that you do not touch than overdoing it. Remember, go slow. To increase little by little is a great approach to take. From there, watch God work. Faith means we trust God for the rest. You may not see how and when it is going to happen. But when you get your tithing in operation and your mind on the kingdom and being financial free, that is when the supernatural will step in and take over. After you build the immediate emergency fund of one month of expenses than any savings after that should go to the 6-8 months of expenses. You can decide to put these in two different accounts, but if you are one of those (I do not trust banks people) then find a safe deposit box or a safe where the money is secure.

Close your eyes and envision every financial need you have in your life is met in abundance. Think about how no one is calling your house, sending you letters, calling your references looking for you and harassing you daily. Think about how you just open the mail and pay any bill at once without thinking about it. Open your eyes. God is taking you to that place. You can get on the path by learning how to start saving today and recognize that as I limit my expenses I can save more and give more. As you give more, God will continue to bless you financially which will allow you to repeat the cycle of saving more and giving more. I challenge you the same way God has challenged me, learn how to save. Learn how to set money aside for emergencies. Learn, if you have a ministry, to get your church in a better position by saving more and reducing the overhead. Experience financial peace and eliminate ongoing stress and worry. God wants you to take His yoke and not your yoke. For His yoke is easy and His burden is light. Start saving.

D: Destroy Debt

"Owe no man anything, but to love one another: for he that loveth another hath fulfilled the law." **Romans 13:8**

Pastor Creflo Dollar wrote a powerful book years ago entitled, "No More Debt." Below are several of his get out of debt principles that I believe are worthy of sharing:

Debt- Something owed to another, or, the condition of owing, to be in debt. Money owed to someone.

How do I get out of debt?

1. **Vision**

You must be able to envision yourself debt free. **Proverbs 29:18** says, "Where there is no vision, the people perish…"

2. Study

Diligently studying the Word of God and studying what His Word has to say concerning debt cancellation.

3. Confession

Write down several scriptures concerning debt cancellation and prosperity. Recite aloud these scriptures daily. Confess to yourself daily that you are "Blessed and that you have plenty more to put in store".

4. Goals:

Write down your financial goals. Develop a plan to achieve these goals. Pray that God helps you to achieve your goals daily.

5. Time:

Allot time to organize and review your household finances. It is recommended that this is done daily. However, this should be done at least once per week.

6. Tithe & Offerings:

Pay your tithes and offerings into a Word-based church. The tithe should be 10% of your gross and the offering should be whatever the Spirit of God directs you to give.

7. Sow:

Sow into the life of your leader or an anointed man or women or God. Sow into the life of someone else who is in debt. This plants the seed of debt release in your life.

8. Mind:

Guard your heart and mind against negative thoughts and attacks from the enemy. Begin to thank God beforehand of the debt release in your life.

9. Obedience:

Obey God in every other area of your life, as well. You do not want your debt release to be hindered by your disobedience in other areas of your life.

10. Focus:

Always stay focused on your goal to be debt free. Keep the mission for wealth at the forefront of your thinking.

Debt is a demon from the pit of hell. Many people continue to stay connected to this demon by adding more and more debt in their lives; bigger houses, bigger cars, bigger sanctuaries, bigger diamonds, bigger colleges, etc. All these things are great, but not if they are at the expense of your future by going into debt. Debt mortgages your future. You'll want to do something down the road, but you can't because you are in debt. Your debt to income ratio is out of proportion. You have become house poor or car poor. All your money is tied up into things. You may live in a million-dollar home but have $20 in your pocket. I met a guy who owned 20 properties and barely made anything from these properties because he had mortgaged most of the properties to finance his premium lifestyle. So, he had all these houses and stuff, but barely had any liquid cash. If there is one thing that I have learned as a real estate investor, is there is nothing that can compare to cash in hand. One bird in hand is always better than two in the bush. When you have cash and no debt then you can tell your cash what to do. Our problem is that we have so much debt that every time we get any money, our debt tells us what we are going to do.

God has pushed me to eliminate every debt in my own life. Debt is not of God and that is why the Bible tells us to owe no man anything. The borrower will always be servant to the lender and until you realize that you will never be able to operate in God's system. In the world's system, they want you to borrow. They make you think that the only way to get a house or a car or go to college is debt. That is not God's system. God does not want anything to have a say in your life other than the Word of God. Debt kills, debt ruins, debt causes stress, debt causes divorces, debt causes people to form addictions, debt causes people to steal, debt causes people to commit suicide, debt causes people to lose their mind and to lose hope. What is debt doing to you? For some of us, you have too much pride to admit you have a problem. You feel too embarrassed to let some of your items go. Financial freedom is more important than the court of public opinion. I would rather everyone laugh at me but have no debt and have money in the bank. Financial freedom allows you to sleep well at night. When you do not have debt, you are "free to move about the kingdom". You can give without reservations. You can give without hesitations. You can live without frustrations. You can have godly motivations.

Benjamin Franklin said, I'd "rather go to bed supperless, than rise in debt." You must attack debt as if it was termites eating away at the foundation of your house. You must treat debt as a malignant cancer that is trying to take your life. So how do you get out of debt? As you go through your expenses, you should be including your debts. You may not be in position to pay off all the debts at once or even pay on all them every month. Depending on the situation, you can start with the smallest or the most pressing (you may have bill collectors calling you nonstop) but determine where to start. In addition, use wisdom when setting up payment plans. I have paid $5 or $10 per month when that was all I had. One thing that I learned is paying something is better than nothing. It shows effort. Other creditors, especially if it is an attorney's office, may not give you much leeway. Do not avoid your creditors, contact them and at least see what you owe and if you have an opportunity for a settlement offer. Avoiding your creditors and watching your mail pile up will not solve anything. Getting out of debt may feel like an overwhelming task at first, but if you get motivated and put all your energy and extra resources into eliminating debt, you will change your attitude about it.

When I was getting out of debt, I made a list of the bills I paid off and kept track of where I was and how long it would take. There is nothing like paying off a bill and moving on to the next. After you pay off a bill, do not use that extra cash to go shopping or to go back into debt, take that money and apply it to the next bill.

Example: Let's say you were paying $50 per month on a bill and you finally got it paid off, when you are done, take this $50 and add it to the amount you are already paying on another bill. This will help to accelerate your debt freedom. The formula to getting out of debt is reducing your expenses and creating more income. The more money you make, the more you can apply it to paying off your debts. As you are paying off debts, it is critical not to increase your expenses. I cannot tell you the quantity of people who have had a paid off car and traded it in for a car with a note. I have been guilty of this myself and have regretted doing it. See we are conditioned to get into debt and to chase stuff. The problem is, we get a temporary high from that material thing, but it is ever fleeting. The moment that note is due or the bill is due, you begin to experience buyer's remorse.

Debt cannot stay in your house. For some of you, debt has moved in and has its own room. You are eating dinner on a table that is financed, sitting on a couch that is financed, watching a TV that is financed, have cars in the garage that are financed and as a result, your future is financed. Because of debt, you must determine what you can and cannot do. Even when you come into some extra money, you must turn it right over to the creditors. Debt is death. Debt is a suffocating spirit that has a bag around your head and is taking the oxygen out of your life. Debt is not your friend. It may be the American way, but it is not God's way. God's way is that you do not have anything in your life that will keep you from serving Him completely. It's hard to have one foot in the kingdom and the other with the bill collectors. People say how God is first in their life, but I would challenge them in that theory. James Frick said, "Do not tell me where your priorities are. Show me where you spend your money, and I'll tell you what they are." I would argue that Walmart and your creditors are more of a priority than the God you say you serve. Where your treasure is, there will be your heart also, so where is your treasure. Compare what you give to the creditors and what you give to God. **Psalm 37:21** tell us that, "The wicked borrows and does not pay back, But the righteous is gracious and gives."

What Christians miss is that when we do not pay what we owe or our slack concerning our promises, then we fall into the category of the wicked. If you want to make your stomach turn, then read in the Bible how God feels about the wicked. We can block our own blessing by giving our tithes but not paying our creditors. We must have integrity when it comes to our finances. I teach my son daily that character means doing what is right. You can stand up and testify how you have been tithing for 30 years but testify about how you have been paying your bills on time or you do not duck and dodge people you owe! As my Archbishop James H. Howell says, "a hush fell over Jerusalem." Henry Ward Beecher said that, "a church's debt is the devil's salary." As I conclude this section on debt, I want to take a moment to urge the pastors reading this to keep their church out of debt.

In 2008, when I was graduating from seminary, my faculty advisor, Dr. Joseph Umidi, gave me some practical and wise pastoral advice. He said get your people and church out of debt, the quicker the better, so they can realize their purpose. When your people and the ministry are burdened down with the weight of debt, your ministry will always be in Lodebar instead of being in the king's palace. I have seen churches build multimillion dollar buildings only to watch people stop giving and for that ministry to go into foreclosure. Where there is vision, there is also provision. Seek God first before going into debt for anything. Being in the real estate business, I understand how you can leverage debt to free up some liquid cash, so debt can work on your behalf in the right situation. If you decide to go into debt, go with an accelerated plan (as I do in real estate investing) of how it is going to be paid off in record time.

Lastly, if you are in debt, this section is not to condemn you or to add an additional burden on you. I assume that most people reading this book may have some type of debt. My heart is to let you know that God wants you to be free and that He does not want you to become comfortable with where you are. It may seem dark right now, but we serve a God that has brought us into the marvelous light. God wants you to be free more than you can imagine.

And, I too want you to understand that getting out of debt is just as much a spiritual battle as it is a natural one. The enemy will tell you how you will always be in debt or there is no way you can pay that mortgage off before 30 years or you cannot buy that car in cash. As my former Bishop Calvin Hanshaw, Sr. used to say, "Whatever the devil tells you, you can always believe the opposite."

John 8:44 calls Satan the "father of lies." He will try to come against you but remember that no weapon formed against you will prosper. Be encouraged, God loves you and regardless of how deep the ditch you have gotten yourself into or the magnitude of your circumstances, God is with you and He will deliver you. Do your part and He will do exceeding abundantly above what you can ask or even think.

O: Operate above sea level

"But if any provide not for his own, and especially for those of his own house, he hath denied the faith, and is worse than an infidel." **1 Timothy 5:8**

One of my favorite all-time money books is "The Richest Man In Babylon" by George Clason. One of the quotes in his book says, "You first learned to live upon less than you earn…" You must learn this first as a kingdom principle and a basic principle to life. You cannot live at what I call sea level or below. Sea level is breaking even, (scenario 2) where you only have enough. Living below sea level is where you are drowning in financial turmoil. I heard one man say that Satan will allow us to keep one nostril above water. The enemy wants you to stay in debt and live below sea level where you are drowning and struggling to "get your head above water." Or, as the theme song of Good Times said, "Keepin' your head above water, making a way if you can." The basis of operating above sea level is simply put, spend less than you earn. Ideally, you want to live off 70% max of what you bring home. When you are living above sea level then you are operating in a place of more than enough and do not feel suffocated by financial pressure.

Craig Hill shared the concept of 5 ancient wealth secrets and gave the following ratio of what to do with your money and how to live above sea level:

1. Tithes: 10%
2. Offerings: 10%
3. Savings: 10%
4. Investing: 20%
5. Spending: 50%

Based on this model, which I am in complete agreement with, we should live off half of what we take in. I have heard some crazy comments and teachings over the years. Even people saying, "I am going to give 90% tithes and live off the 10%". That statement may be good for preaching, but that is not accurate.

Tithing is 10% and anything above and beyond that is an offering. In this case, mentioned by Craig Hill, he uses this principle to teach people, especially children, how to manage money and spend less than they earn at a young age. The issue in our society is that we are raising our children on debt and passing on a legacy of not enough. We focus more on getting our credit score up instead of getting your savings up. Here is a tip, if you have enough money, you will not ever need credit. Credit is designed for the world's system, so they can put a value on what you are worth and capable of financially. But money talks, I am not going to say *what walks,* but you get the picture. If you see a house you want and write a check and pay for it in cash, no one is going to ask for a preapproval letter or your credit score. In God's system, everyone is approved!

Spend less than you make. What a timeless principle. You cannot spend more than you make, yet people do it all the time. Praying the check clears your bank or making payments when you know you do not have the funds in the bank. Your lifestyle is pulling you further and further under water. In God's system, you are not drowning from being overextended or even stuck in just enough, you are always way above sea level. This "just keeping my head above water mentality" is from the pit of hell. Poverty and lack are the devil's work and needs to be sent right back to hell.

Your goal, at a minimum, should live off 70% of your income for household expenses. Everything else should go to giving, saving, investing, etc. As Craig Hill mentioned, to move into the realm of wealth, you want to drive this number down to 50%. Think about being able to put that much money into savings, investing, and giving generously every single paycheck. Your financial situation would change in one month or even one day! We cannot continue the vicious cycle of borrowing from Peter to pay Paul. After a while, you are going to owe Peter, Paul, and Mary. I submit to you the greatest challenge of becoming financially independent is not tithing but learning how to faithfully manage the 90%. Your tithing cannot correct the hot mess you have created by mismanagement of the 90%. You must be a steward of all. Tithing helps to rebuke the devourer, but you continue to invite the devourer back by poor money choices.

When someone is cut, the first thing you must do is stop the bleeding. After you start tithing, learn how to properly manage the 90%. I have given you an abundance of spiritual and natural principles, but do not stop there, Read, read and read some more. Even get a copy of my second book, "Biblical Principles For Entrepreneurs". There, I share over 100+ scriptures on finances and entrepreneurship. You can also order a copy of this book on our website: *www.empowerlives.net*.

You must become a student of your finances to truly show yourself approved to be able to handle more. When you are living in abundance and well above sea level, you will understand and experience the true peace and freedom of God. God wants us to operate above sea level so that we can reach down and pull up everyone that we see drowning. Prosperity is not just for you to get the fourth Cadillac, but to help pull others out of the dark.

The greatest gift you can give someone is a hand up and guide them into the truth of God's will for provision in their own life. Each one, teach one. Teach others how to live prosperously. Meaning people do not prosper to the full extent that God intended because they become so selfish and self-centered, that God has no reason to continue to bless them over and above what they already have. Overflow is for people who want to help others get out of lack, poverty, debt, and stress.

People spend their whole lives paying bills and some never realize that God had so much more for them than what was due on the 1st of the month. Do not allow the rat race of life to blind you from what God is trying to do. You may be living below sea level now and feel like you are drowning, but the good news is that we have a lifeguard called Jesus Christ who can save you. Who the Son sets free is free indeed. Jesus died so you can be free from this mess. Accepting Him means accepting His ways and how he operates. Do not just recognize Him on Sunday but more importantly, recognize Him in your money. I have learned in this process that sometimes you have to break down and get on your knees and say, "God teach me thy ways and show me how to get out of this mess." As the quartet group, the Canton Spirituals said, "I gotta clean up what I messed up." Sometimes you must start where you are to get where God is taking you. Be encouraged and learn to live below your means so that you can enjoy life above sea level!

M: Master Money

"Be diligent to know the state of your flocks, and attend to your herds" **Proverbs 27:23**

Becoming a master at anything takes time and discipline. Whether it is chess or karate, it takes practice and a continual study of your craft. When we examine our own finances, we may have discovered that money has mastered us. If your money is always telling you what to do and what bills you must pay before you do anything else, then yes, it has mastered you.

Galatians 4:7 says, "Therefore you are no longer a slave, but a son; and if a son, then an heir through God." Since we are no longer slaves, but sons and heirs to the throne, then why are we still trying to go back into slavery? When we allow money to master us by staying in debt or tolerating lack, then we are truly slaves. **Galatians 2:18** tells us that, "For if I build again the things which I destroyed, I make myself a transgressor." We cannot continue to build again what God has destroyed in our lives.

Let me give you 4 steps to master money as God has given them to me to share with you:

1. Set time aside weekly (daily in the beginning) to review your budget and to find any areas that you can make tweaks. Always pray before you start and ask for God wisdom.
2. Limit the times you do things outside of your budget (ex. Quick trip to the store, eating out, etc.) These are budget killers. I remember one month I planned $400 on groceries and spent $1000!
3. Put the extra or unexpected money to your savings and paying off debts, after you tithe. Whether someone blesses you with some cash, tax refund, etc., put it towards savings and debts. Extra cash is a blessing and it is easy to get the "spirit of spend" on you when you get it. Discipline is the name of this game.
4. Be thankful; live in expectation and maintain your joy. On this journey, I have learned that thanksgiving will always increase our capacity for more. Look at the boy with the two-piece fish dinner. Jesus took what He had, and the Bible says that He gave thanks. After He gave thanks He fed thousands. In addition, learn how to live in expectation. Debt may have you down now, but God is going to bring you out and you

must believe that and expect that! Lastly, the hardest part of this journey is to maintain your joy. As someone said, that it is our job to maintain what Jesus obtained. Keep your joy full even if your bank account is empty.

God's Promise

CHAPTER 7

"And Elijah came unto all the people, and said, how long halt ye between two opinions? If the LORD be God, follow him: but if Baal, then follow him. And the people answered him not a word." **1 Kings 18:21**

In this passage of scripture, we understand that Elijah is having a showdown with the prophets of Baal and he challenges the people to choose which God they will serve; the one true God or Baal. As you read in the text, Elijah challenged them to call on their God and bring fire down from heaven. He even joked about them because they could not call down fire from heaven. See the world's system cannot create the real thing, it can only produce a counterfeit. Ultimately, the one true God reigned down fire and in verse 40, Elijah killed all of these prophets and not one of them escaped. To walk in God's promise, you must kill everything in your life that is a part of the world's system. God's promise is that when you commit to His system 100%, then He will make a clear distinction between you and the world. There was a clear distinction between Elijah and the prophets of Baal. The issue we have today is that Christians have become so mired in the clay of the world that you almost must take a spiritual DNA test to determine the saved person from the unsaved person. When you blend the world with God's system, you only get a mess. Sometimes it is hard for us to see all the promises that God has for us.

Here is a powerful prayer to pray **Ephesians 1:18** "The eyes of your understanding being enlightened; that ye may know the hope of his calling, and the riches of the glory of his inheritance in the saints". Elisha in **2 Kings 6:16-17** when being surrounded by the Syrian army and his servant was having an anxiety attack, he had to pray, "Fear not: for they that be with us are more than they that be with them. And Elisha prayed, and said, LORD, I pray thee, open his eyes, that he may see. And the LORD opened the eyes of the young man; and he saw: and, behold, the mountain was full of horses and chariots of fire round about Elisha." When God opens our spiritual eyes, we can truly see what He has for us.

God birthed this book in me for such a time as this. The body of Christ has been suffering and in bondage to mammon far too long. I believe that God will help me get this book into the hands of at least 1 million people who want to Get Off The System. It vexes my spirit to see people struggle financially and wonder how they will feed their kids or keep the lights on. This is what keeps me up at night. How can I help people recognize that God has a better way and a better system?

Get Off The System: Moving From Lack To Abundance, is in essence, a farewell letter to Satan and the world's system. I charge you today to write your own farewell letter to the world's system. I have always subscribed to the notion that once we know better, we will do better. Now, you know better and it is time for you to do better. You cannot change what you constantly tolerate. You can longer tolerate not enough, lack and insufficiency in your life. If you are under pressure right now, be encouraged. When I used to lift weights in high school, my football coach would add more weight to the bar to help me build more muscle. So, if you are under pressure, use that weight to build the spiritual fortitude you need to overcome the enemy. You will never possess what you are willing to pursue. You must pursue getting off the system with everything you have. Your mind must shift. Your mind will either build you a prison or palace. My wife and I will be praying with you as you navigate through your financial journey to get off the system.

Mark this book up, highlight, crease the pages and read it again. At the end of this chapter, I have included a daily confession that you can repeat daily to speak over your finances. Do not just say it but get it into your spirit until you believe it and see yourself financially free. We are sowing the seeds of faith from this book into your life, so you can reap a harvest of financial independence and wealth to be used for the kingdom of God. You also can be a blessing to us and sow into our lives and ministry by doing the following 5 items:

1. Get 10 people to order a copy or purchase 10 copies to give away *(www.empowerlives.net)*
2. Start a small group that focuses on discussing this book and getting off the system. I am willing to call in and do a welcome call to get everyone started.
3. Post a book review on amazon and other book review sites.
4. Invite Alton Jamison to your church to teach on how to get off the system and move from lack to abundance. *(www.empowerlives.net)*

5. Email us your testimonies (use the contact form on www.empowerlives.net) of the breakthroughs you have received after applying the principles in this book.

Visit our website: *www.empowerlives.net* and you can order additional books, contact our office about bringing me and/or my wife in to speak at your church or event and view other products and books that we have available. As I conclude, I leave you with a powerful daily confession to repeat and with these words from Martin Luther King, Jr., "only in darkness can you see the stars." You may feel like you are in darkness financially, but the bright and Morning Star by the name of Jesus Christ will lead you to the light. Be empowered!

Daily financial confession

In the name of Jesus, I declare my days of lack and not enough are over. I will no longer struggle and live from check to check. The noose of debt is removed from around my neck. The stronghold of poverty is destroyed. The yoke of lack is broken once and for all. God is my source. I renounce mammon and the systems of the world and my allegiance to them. I repent for the sins of my father and mother and previous generations concerning finances and the mishandling of money. Close any door in my bag, fix any breach and fill any crack. I walk in supernatural favor and blessing. My household is blessed. My family is blessed and my children (if you have any) are blessed. I have the anointing of a good steward and I will establish boundaries in my finances and will no longer be influenced by the lust of the eyes, the lust of the flesh and the pride of life when making financial decisions. My bills are paid in full, I have no mortgage, student loans, credit card debts, medical bills, car notes or any debts. I am righteous and not wicked. I will fix any wrong that I have done financially. God is my source and I will not fear what man can do to me. I am a tither and a giver, and I live in constant overflow. I am above and not beneath. I am the head and not the tail. Daily I walk in the fullness of God's purposes and promises in my life. I will not quit until I see the enemy defeated in my finances and in my life. And I will not quit until I see the goodness of the Lord in the land of the living. Millionaire and Billionaire status is mine. I am a kingdom financier and money is no longer my master but my servant. I am blessed to be a blessing. I am now resting in Him and I have and receive financial peace and I am finally free in Jesus name, Amen!

About the Author

Alton originates from Hopewell, VA. He obtained his Bachelor of Science degree in Mechanical Engineering Technology from Old Dominion University and was recognized in Who's Who Among Students in American Universities and Colleges. He obtained his Master of Arts in Practical Theology from Regent University and completed courses to become a certified Life and Success Coach through Transformational Leadership Coaching. He is currently pursuing a Doctorate in Education in Organizational Leadership from Grand Canyon University. He is a two time-International Speech Contest Champion (District Level) hosted by Toastmasters International. A successful entrepreneur, he is the owner of several businesses. Alton was recognized by Inside Business Journal, as one of the Top Forty under 40 in Hampton Roads, VA.

Alton's creative ability also carries over into print. His work has been featured in several books, "Rekindling the Human Spirit: That is My Story and I'm Sticking To It" and "Brother To Brother-Motivation For Young African American Men." In addition, his inspirational memoir "No More Handcuffs: 5 Keys To Removing The Mental Handcuffs From Your Life!" He is also the author of "Biblical Principles For Entrepreneurs" and the co-author, with his wife, of "Purpose, Passion & Prosperity: 3 Keys To A Godly Marriage".

Currently he is the Pastor of The Empowerment Zone, a Church Plant in the City of Baton Rouge, LA. However, his greatest accomplishment is marrying his college math tutor, TaShawnda Jamison, and together they have two beautiful children, Madison and Joshua.

Alton speaks globally! If you are interested in having him and/or his wife, TaShawnda at your next conference or event, please visit: *www.empowerlives.net* or call us directly at 225-271-2019.

www.ingramcontent.com/pod-product-compliance
Lightning Source LLC
Chambersburg PA
CBHW060602100426
42744CB00008B/1279